Open Data for Everybody

What if I told you something that could empower our third sector and activists to enhance their capacity? From gathering evidence for funding tenders to campaigning for crucial social issues and much more? It's called open data, yet many in social action remain unaware of it. Primarily shaped by corporate entities, open data seems tailored only for technologists, alienating the third sector. But in reality, it's a powerful tool for social change, bolstering civil society, and creating resilient communities.

This book argues a simple point: if open data and the digital aspects that support it aren't accessible to all, then what is the point of it? In an age where technology should be seen as a fundamental human right, it's time to rethink outreach. Deeply rooted in grassroots social activism, this book explores a journey that led to collaboration with governments globally, based on real hands-on work, aiming to democratize open data. Through narrative storytelling, we share insights, best practices, procedures, and community-driven approaches. Regardless of your skill set or organization size, from grassroots workers to third-sector professionals and government officers, join us to reshape the perception of open data, fostering change in neighborhoods.

Open Data for Everybody: Using Open Data for Social Good is a love letter to open data's transformative power. To create solutions, understanding the problem is crucial. This book seeks to return control to the real experts—those living and working within our communities.

Open Data for Everybody
Using Open Data for Social Good

Nathan Coyle

CRC Press
Taylor & Francis Group
Boca Raton London New York

CRC Press is an imprint of the
Taylor & Francis Group, an **informa** business
A CHAPMAN & HALL BOOK

Designed cover image: Nathan Coyle

First edition published 2024
by CRC Press
2385 NW Executive Center Drive, Suite 320, Boca Raton FL 33431

and by CRC Press
4 Park Square, Milton Park, Abingdon, Oxon, OX14 4RN

CRC Press is an imprint of Taylor & Francis Group, LLC

© 2024 Nathan Coyle

Library of Congress Cataloging-in-Publication Data
Names: Coyle, Nathan, author.
Title: Open data for everybody : using open data for social good / Nathan Coyle.
Description: First edition. | Boca Raton, FL : Taylor & Francis Group, 2024. |
Includes bibliographical references.
Identifiers: LCCN 2023056547 (print) | LCCN 2023056548 (ebook) |
ISBN 9781032724621 (hbk) | ISBN 9781032715049 (pbk) | ISBN 9781032724645 (ebk)
Subjects: LCSH: Technological innovation—Social aspects.
Classification: LCC HC79.T4 C697 2024 (print) | LCC HC79.T4 (ebook) |
DDC 303.48/34—dc23/eng/20240324
LC record available at https://lccn.loc.gov/2023056547
LC ebook record available at https://lccn.loc.gov/2023056548

ISBN: 978-1-032-72462-1 (hbk)
ISBN: 978-1-032-71504-9 (pbk)
ISBN: 978-1-032-72464-5 (ebk)

DOI: 10.1201/9781032724645

Typeset in Times
by codeMantra

Access the Workshop Manuscript: www.routledge.com/9781032715049

Contents

About the Author

Nathan Coyle is a British digital activist, former Director of a leading civic innovation organization, and currently leads the Peace Technology at the Austrian Centre for Peace in Vienna. With a wealth of international experience, Nathan has partnered with governments across the globe, both local and central, to enhance their digital outreach efforts, employing innovative strategies such as hackathons, toolkit design, civic tech, and human-centered design. He has conducted talks and lectures across Europe on the subject of making open data and smart cities more accessible, including a TEDx talk, and has written for various publications such as the Huffington Post, The Guardian, and Vice Media. He is also a keen developer and graphic designer, who tried to instill creativity in every aspect of policy design.

Introduction

1

From the very first moment I learned about open data, quite a while ago now, I was immediately struck by the misconceptions surrounding it. It didn't take long before I started to question why open data had acquired such a misleading narrative. Despite the best intentions, this narrative had been shaped by the wrong individuals.

I am a fervent advocate for tech for good. Although I have held various roles in civic technology throughout my career, ranging from design to directorship, I primarily identify as a community developer and a social activist. I have consistently seen open data's potential to be accessible and user-friendly, and I've challenged senior figures to reconsider painting it in a corporate light. My passion lies in changing that perception, and I hope you'll join me in sharing this vision.

While digital tools are undeniably crucial for capacity building, it's essential to remember that technology, in itself, is not the ultimate solution. It merely serves as a means to document and provide evidence of our work, whether we're utilizing the data we collect or sharing content on social media. Technology is the conduit for collecting evidence, not the physical work that brings about positive change in the world—that's what you do.

What's crucial is that our processes remain human-centered. It's time for open data to align itself with this principle, work on improving its image, and create a lasting, meaningful impact for our third sector. Moreover, it should have the capability to activate activists, which I firmly believe it can achieve.

Technology is absolutely pointless unless it is accessible.

For those who may not be familiar, open data refers to the idea that certain information should be shared, freely available, and replicable without charge. In my opinion, it serves as a tool for collaboration, enabling anyone to access datasets released by governments, international organizations, non-profits, research institutions, and crowdsourced platforms on an ever-growing range of topics such as water supply, housing supply, making your environment more climate-friendly, and much more.

If these datasets are not readily available, it becomes crucial for people to recognize the role open data can play in advancing toward a free and fair society. Through your advocacy, individuals can challenge governments and larger organizations to release more data. To support this effort, it is important to develop a narrative that resonates with everyone and highlights the uses and importance of open data and acquiring skills to hold decision-makers accountable, persuading them to make data openly accessible.

However, for those unfamiliar with open data or who have heard professionals and academics discuss it in the past, it may seem like an impenetrable subject. I aim to use

DOI: 10.1201/9781032724645-1

this book as a means to rethink how we communicate open data and stay true to its original concept. My goal is to articulate it clearly and simply, dispelling myths and decoding the unnecessary hype surrounding it.

Even if you consider yourself an open data expert, I believe there is still something to be learned from this book. After reading it, I encourage you to pass it on to grassroots organizations in your area and urge them to read it. This book is written in a style that community activists will understand, reflecting my own perspective as a social change actor. We think differently from the corporate and academic sectors, and this difference poses one of the challenges.

In this book, I will explain open data using a storytelling narrative. I will delve into why open data has been portrayed in a certain light, not just to fill pages but to understand why. Regardless of whether you are a policymaker, public servant, NGO worker, or activist, I believe it is a conversation we should all be having with each other, especially when open data has the genuine potential to bring about change.

I will also frequently reference COVID-19 as an example and what it has taught us. From funding to misinformation, the pandemic brought many issues to the surface—things that we have had to face head-on. It has offered us valuable learning opportunities that will help us analyze issues for decades to come.

Throughout this publication, I will frequently use the term "third sector" as a catch-all term encompassing charity, voluntary sector organizations, activities, and general community projects.

To provide some context, this work has been developed through a series of trainings, workshops, hackathons, and research projects conducted worldwide. I have collaborated with partners such as the HM UK Government, the Federal Government of the United States, the Federal Government of Germany, the Government of Kenya, the Scottish Government, the Government of Colombia, the Palestinian Authority, the Government of the Slovak Republic, the Government of the Czech Republic, the Government of Romania, the Dominican Republic Government, and local government partners including the State Government of Ontario in Canada and the City Government of São Paulo in Brazil, as well as various city government partners across the UK and Germany.

I have also collaborated with numerous think tanks in Europe, including the Bertelsmann Stiftung in Germany, and a wide range of NGOs, from large organizations to small volunteer-led grassroots initiatives in our community.

I mention these entities not to boast but to provide credibility to the fact that this book is based on an actual formula rather than the musings of a random activist without foundation. A significant amount of work has gone into gathering genuine samples and evidence on the issue to produce this book.

As I draw upon my previous experiences, I also strive to reflect on my own upbringing and the time spent working in some of the most marginalized areas in the UK. These encounters have not only offered insights into how NGOs operate but have also granted me a firsthand understanding of the immense significance of charities. Growing up in a family that relied on their support to get by, I deeply recognize their importance, fueling my fervent advocacy to encourage everyone to offer their utmost support to these vital projects.

Furthermore, I want to reflect personally as someone who comes from what some may consider a person originating from an economically disadvantaged area. I have witnessed firsthand the impact that NGOs can have on real people's lives. These organizations understand the issues at the grassroots level because it's their own community too. That's why I am so passionate about how open data can genuinely support community development and enable these projects to continue their excellent work.

I genuinely hope that my narrative, rooted in having experienced both sides of the coin—from being part of and working with organizations that tackle poverty to assisting central governments in improving outreach to the third sector—will provide a comprehensive perspective on the critical role of charities and their profound impact on society.

To be clear, whilst I conceived the original concept of this outreach work, a substantial portion of the feedback has come from real people in the community, professionals, and government sectors. I am sharing a body of evidence with you that may assist in your work or even change your perception of open data. Who knows?

The main objective of this book is to propose a different approach to open data outreach and provide insights into what makes sense to the third sector. If you are an activist or work for an NGO, I hope this book can help you better visualize what open data is, how you can use it, and what you can potentially achieve with it. For policymakers, I hope this book can inspire you to devise mechanisms that involve the local third sector and enable them to utilize your data for social good.

Irrespective of where you stand, I will focus on the narrative of this book on outreach rather than delving into the commercial aspects of open data. I believe this piece of writing will best serve its purpose if it is easily digestible and straightforward, albeit with a touch of commentary.

The central theme of this publication revolves around normal people utilizing open data for social action, not technology experts. As you continue reading, please keep this concept in mind.

Whether you are a government official or worker seeking a different perspective, a third-sector staff member looking to understand open data in a way that makes sense to you, or an activist wanting to learn how to use digital media to hold your local decision-makers accountable, I hope you will find something in here that will be of assistance.

What Is Open Data?

2

The term open data was first coined in 1995 by an American think tank,[1] but the idea of it goes back to the early 1940s, when Robert King Merton described the importance of making the results of research freely accessible to all. He believed that researchers should contribute to the "common pot"[2] and embrace the idea of relinquishing intellectual property rights to foster the advancement of knowledge.

Data connects everybody in the world in some way or another, but something like open data can help us connect our skills and work on issues collaboratively, regardless of whether it's activism, health, or academia. Irrespective of the matter, open data helps us to work on various projects simultaneously, solving real problems, driving innovation, scientific discovery, or even setting up a business based on certain data.

It's a series of zeros and ones that help us to work on projects from all facets of our community ecosystem, collaboratively working together to solve social issues that potentially plague our society. From government corruption, conflict prevention, and water shortages in areas of high poverty to curing diseases, there are endless opportunities and examples.

Living in the 21st century, it is clear that society is becoming more and more dependent on digital, and we have an insatiable desire for new technology. And if you are one of those people who dislike technology, I'm afraid I have bad news for you—it is only going to accelerate. Now, with the debate around how best to introduce artificial intelligence, which at worst will be implemented within the development of sophisticated cybersecurity innovations—something that depends on data—it's not going anywhere anytime soon, and the agenda is not going to change.

You probably don't realize that you are using data right now. Take your phone, for example. Do you check the weather before you leave the house or even on the TV? Perhaps you'll be looking to move home soon. If you have children, would you check out local schools or transport links? Maybe you're considering going to university. How will you compare the cost of your course to a different one? If you're lost, the first thing you'll probably do is take out your phone and open your GPS map app, right? The possibilities are limitless, from tracking your fitness or weight control to planning which bus or train you'll take the next morning.

The answer to all those questions will most likely involve a website or app that uses data to operate and do its job. It is built on data—data that is changing in real time.

DOI: 10.1201/9781032724645-2

Before we continue, let's try to clarify some of the widely used terms so you have a better understanding of what open data looks like in practical terms.

HUMAN-READABLE

This information is presented in a way that the naked eye can understand. Here, we are talking about formats such as PDF, XML, and Doc. Imagine files and all the usual types of things you can send or receive via email. These will mostly consist of reports, database documents, surveys, and photographs.

MACHINE-READABLE DATA

This is a format that your computer can easily read and process in a structured manner as it is stored on a computer disk. It's not meant for us to understand, and it won't make much sense unless you have a good grasp of coding languages. You will need the help of software to make sense of it and crunch all that information into a visualized format. These files include CSV, JSON, and XML. If you download these files and feel overwhelmed by how complicated they look, don't worry—it's not just you.

It is worth mentioning that even though a CSV file is essentially machine-readable, you can open it in the spreadsheet software of your choice and view the data. So, it can tentatively cross over into being human-readable. It is easier for your computer to read, but it is similar to the native spreadsheet file format you are probably more familiar with, such as XML.

The following information may not be as relevant to you, but since we are exploring what open data is without the hyperbole, it will help you understand how it is published.

LICENSING AND OPEN DATA

For data to be considered open data, it needs to be licensed, and there are several ways to do this. However, in line with openness, whether you are downloading or sharing your own open data, you would be looking for an open license.

In most cases, open data is licensed under the Creative Commons framework,[3] which is a public copyright license that allows the free distribution of the work you are releasing. In simpler terms, it is a way to copyright your work while still allowing anyone to access it, change it, or use it as they please, as long as they credit you. It's advisable to use a Creative Commons license, as all the legal work has been done for you. However, you could also research if your local government has its own open licenses. But if you'd like my advice, I would stick with the former. More on this topic will be discussed later.

HOW DATA IS PRESENTED

Data visualization helps us digest information in a way that we can understand, such as through graphs, charts, and infographics. During the COVID-19 pandemic, for example, you would have been accustomed to seeing data presented in this way, regardless of whether it was open or not.

However, it's no secret that data can be manipulated and visualized in a way that tells a certain narrative, which may not strictly be true or may overlook the whole story. This is known as cherry-picking. It involves highlighting specific cases that support a particular viewpoint while ignoring contradictory evidence or alternative data studies that may yield different results.

Cherry-picking is common in the pet food industry, for instance, where large pharmaceutical firms may hire labs to showcase only positive results from trials with cats, dogs, horses, cattle, and sheep using their novel drugs. You might see a TV advertisement stating, "4 out of 5 pets showed health improvement after 2 months with this food." However, if you examine it closely, you'll notice a significant asterisk next to it, indicating a larger study involving a larger number of animals, let's say 20. This means that the improvement could be as low as 4 out of 20 pets.

Another form of cherry-picking that you may come across is the manipulation of data through graphs to make a politician appear more popular than they are. Usually, when people are surveyed, they are given multiple options to choose from. If presented in a pie chart, the percentages may add up to more than 100%, which is inaccurate because a pie chart can only show the proportions of a whole, with each segment adding up to 100%. If individuals surveyed chose more than one person they would vote for, the total would exceed 100%, providing a misleading representation.

OPEN DATA IN GOVERNMENT

You may have heard the term "gov data" or open government data (OGD). This refers to specific information released by a government, whether at the local or national level. It is usually part of a government's open government agenda, demonstrating transparency and commitment to engaging with citizens, institutions, and businesses by inviting them to use the information to improve government services, encourage scrutiny, and promote civic engagement.

All these factors are crucial to understanding the essence of open data, how it is released, and how it is processed.

Data governance and ethics play a vital role in ensuring that open data is used responsibly and ethically. As more and more data is made available, concerns arise regarding privacy, security, and the potential for misuse. Therefore, it is essential to establish robust governance frameworks and adhere to ethical principles to safeguard individuals' rights and maintain public trust.

Open data has the potential to revolutionize various sectors, including government, business, healthcare, and education. By making data accessible and actionable, we can drive innovation, empower citizens, and make informed decisions that have a positive impact on society.

Open data is a powerful concept that promotes transparency, collaboration, and accessibility. It enables us to leverage the wealth of information available to address societal challenges, drive progress, and foster innovation. As we move forward, it is crucial to ensure that open data initiatives are supported by strong governance, ethical considerations, and responsible use, so that we can fully harness the potential of this valuable resource.

To give you an overview, I want to give you some information on open data's cousins, or at least where some of this open data might end up. We won't cover these too much in this book; I want to give you substance on the issue at hand, using open data for social good from more non-technical know-how, but just for informative purposes.

BIG DATA

Big data—sometimes data can get really vast! It is essentially a huge digital repository of information, comprising extensive and intricate datasets that surpass the capacity of conventional data processing tools. It encompasses structured data, often found in databases, as well as unstructured data such as text, images, and real-time sensor readings collected from diverse sources. To extract valuable insights, detect patterns, and uncover trends within these massive datasets, organizations leverage advanced analytical techniques and cutting-edge technologies. Across diverse sectors such as healthcare, finance, marketing, and logistics, big data serves as a pivotal asset for making informed decisions, optimizing operations, and gaining a competitive edge in our data-centric era.

Big data serves as a powerful tool across a diverse array of industries, revolutionizing the way they operate. In pharmaceuticals, it plays a crucial role in crafting individualized treatment strategies. Meanwhile, in the retail sector, big data drives the creation of personalized product recommendations and ensures efficient inventory management. Finance relies on it for credit risk evaluation and the execution of algorithmic trading. Beyond these and sometimes blue-chip sectors, big data's reach extends to traffic management, crime analysis, and energy conservation, to name a few. It helps make informed decisions, elevate their products, and streamline processes, plus, thanks to its powerful enough software to crunch and store it, it is expensive.

However, it's important to note that harnessing the potential of big data often requires delving into data science, which might be less accessible for entry-level individuals without a specific interest in grabbing your lab coat.

LINKED DATA

Linked data is like creating organized digital maps for information on the internet. It's a structured way to make data easier to find and explore online. This method uses standardized technologies, which are like commonly agreed-upon rules and tools that everyone uses, ensuring that different systems and devices can work together seamlessly.

Linked data can create collaboration across diverse fields, looking to establish shared data meanings and seamless connectivity among data sources. For librarians, for example, it involves a fundamental shift in data organization. Instead of retaining data in librarian-centric databases, linked data restructures it into easily comprehensible collections of information about various entities. This approach facilitates easier integration with data from different domains, enhancing the visibility and influence of libraries in interdisciplinary collaborations (Figure 2.1).

Well, now that you know the bigger picture, let's just get into the nitty-gritty of how we can use open data for the betterment of our neighborhoods.

Remember, data is all around us, shaping our daily lives and influencing our choices. Embracing open data and understanding its implications can empower us to navigate the digital landscape effectively and contribute to a more transparent and connected world.

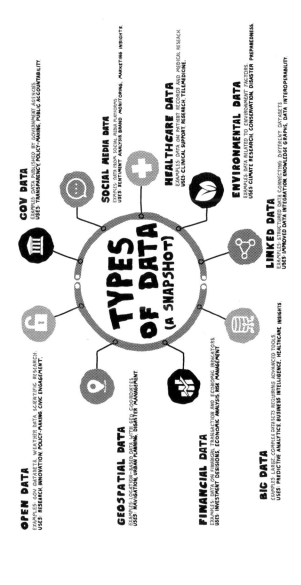

FIGURE 2.1   An overview of the different types of data.

NOTES

1 Lathrop, D., & Ruma, L. (2010). *Open Government*. O'Reilly Media, Inc. ISBN: 9780596804350.
2 Merton, R. K. (1968). *Social Theory and Social Structure* (enlarged ed.). ISBN: 9780029211304.
3 Creative Commons. (n.d.). About CC Licenses. https://creativecommons.org/about/cclicenses/

From the Ground Up

3

Using Open Data to Help Close the Digital Divide

Even though open data is machine-made, it has roots in very real processes and consequences that affect real people's lives, both working and personal, so why not explain it in that way? Setting data narratives that outline the meaning of the data helps normal people visualize in their heads how they can use it for their usage, no matter how obvious the dataset is.

Sometimes it is not just skills that can hold us back; it is the technology that we have access to.

In today's world, I see access to technology as a human right and not a luxury. As our lives become increasingly digital, this shapes our ability to exercise our social, economic, cultural, and political rights. However, the benefits of digitalization are highly uneven, making it clear that we need more people who have the vision to challenge existing practices and the skills to produce inclusive innovation to ensure that nobody is left behind.

Addressing the digital divide remains a persistent challenge for local governments and social housing providers worldwide. To bridge this gap, they frequently collaborate with NGOs to tackle the issue head-on. As essential services increasingly transition to digital platforms, it becomes imperative for individuals, including those relying on social security benefits, to acquire the digital skills necessary for tasks such as bill payments and reporting services. The need for digital upskilling is evident. While many regional institutions engage in these efforts, it's crucial to recognize that their motivation extends beyond goodwill; they aim to empower residents with the capabilities to manage rent payments and navigate digital processes effectively (Figure 3.1).

In keeping this in mind, the stark reality is that gaining access to technology remains a pressing problem, particularly outside of the Western world, though not limited to it. Having personally witnessed this while working in disadvantaged areas by UK

DOI: 10.1201/9781032724645-3

FIGURE 3.1   How does the digital divide affect the people who live in our communities?

standards, various factors such as social, geographical, and geopolitical criteria act as mitigating circumstances, making the issue even more challenging to address.

Even in refugee camps in some of the most volatile places on earth, some of these areas may not have running water, but you will be sure to see smartphones.[1]

What we all need to embed into our psyche is that technology is no longer just a necessity; it is integrated into modern society, regardless if that is something we think is a good thing or not.

This reality became increasingly apparent during the pandemic, when we relied extensively on technology for various aspects of our lives. From remote work to every-day grocery shopping and even virtual social gatherings, technology played a pivotal role. In the UK, the concept of a "Virtual Pub" where friends would meet online for a drink gained prominence.

The shift to online education was another noteworthy development. It wasn't lim-ited to university students transitioning to digital learning, often at substantial costs for tuition and accommodation. The true impact was felt among younger children attempt-ing to maintain their regular learning routines. It's here that the digital divide among households became palpable.

If anything it intensified digital exclusion and poverty, in the UK, in households that are already in deprivation, it was clear and sometimes it was a choice to be able to pay the Wi-Fi bill so their children can access education and learn, or feed them,[2] as reported by the University of Cambridge—this highlights how inequality is not just physical; in the modern online world, it's digital too.

A report from the International Telecommunication Union and UNICEF stated that "two-thirds of the world's school-age children have no internet access at home."[3] To put that into perspective for you, that is 1.3 billion children aged 3–17 years old, worldwide.

To a lot of us, having access to this technology, good Wi-Fi, and hardware is a privi-lege and not a necessity; we just do not see that a lot of the time.

Grassroots NGOs are typically run by low-paid workers or volunteers, often relying on donated old computers. However, the good news is that outdated technology does not hinder the use of open data. Old or inexpensive technology suffices when internet usage is the main requirement. Moreover, as we will touch on later in the book, there is an abundance of free open-source software available for word processing and spreadsheet viewing. Nevertheless, accessing the internet remains an expensive endeavor.

In 2017, the Office for National Statistics, the UK's largest independent producer of official statistics, reported that the Black Country in England,[4] where my hometown resides, had one of the lowest rates of internet usage in the entire UK. Community groups were already aware of this data, as the rise in people using food banks indicated that families primarily spent their limited resources on necessities rather than tech-nology. To address this issue, many charities established digital cafés where residents could access technology, learn about the internet, and even borrow laptops and tablets temporarily.

Reflecting on my personal experience, I grew up in a household where we had similar experiences; there were times when we had to choose between buying food or paying household bills. I have witnessed firsthand the struggles faced by families and the guilt they feel about providing their children with the same opportunities as their friends or what they perceive their friends to have. I do not want families to endure such hardships. I must admit, I am grateful that finding data on digital usage, food poverty, fuel poverty, and education is relatively easy. In my own small way, no matter how local it may be, I strive to make a difference. This is precisely why I am so passionate about using open data for social good. I genuinely believe that grassroots community organizations are the most effective means of bringing about tangible change for real people in our neighborhoods.

This deep passion for open data has driven me to dedicate a significant portion of my career to deconstructing and promoting its importance. Open data enables us to illustrate the implications of the digital divide with facts and evidence. However, those who reside in the affected areas and genuinely care about the issues, people, and places can provide additional context. We can utilize this data to weave a narrative and contextualize social issues in a manner that resonates with our fellow citizens. Above all, we can offer a storytelling narrative that garners support and encourages participation. When it comes to uniting people, especially in marginalized communities, it is our grassroots, voluntary, and civil organizations that play a crucial role.

I wanted to use this example to underscore the humanitarian aspect of technology in everyday life. If societal gaps undermine community resilience, data can paint a vivid picture that we can use to address this, but only if we can collectively activate people to seek it out and use it.

However, if our third sector can provide context and propose solutions that are more likely to succeed, we must explore that path. Why? Because it is their neighborhood, their home, and their heart. If a project, campaign, or event is to be successful, they are best equipped to facilitate it and engage the community.

One could argue that these organizations are indispensable, and I would wholeheartedly agree. This brings us back to the question of how we can ensure they have the resources needed to progress, expand, and, as we mentioned before, simply exist.

Now, we must make a compelling case for civil society organizations to become more astute and smart. They must operate with increased agility, and using data to inform their decisions can support that.

Training grassroots NGO workers to harness the potential of open data is a crucial step toward empowering them to tackle local challenges effectively, as it will help them to really understand where they work in cold, hard facts. The first order of business is to conduct a thorough assessment of the current state of data-related skills within these communities. This entails considering factors such as literacy levels, preferred languages, and access to technology, all of which play a pivotal role in tailoring the training to meet their specific needs.

In response to these findings, the development of customized training programs comes next. These programs should start at the very beginning, instilling the fundamentals of data literacy. Workers need to grasp the essentials of data collection, organization, and interpretation, often best facilitated through basic tools such as spreadsheets. A paramount aspect of this training is instilling a strong sense of ethics and responsibility in data handling, ensuring that privacy and consent considerations are paramount.

But that's just the beginning. The next phase involves equipping these grassroots workers with practical skills in data analysis, visualization, and the art of leveraging open data sources that are directly relevant to their missions. The emphasis here is on hands-on learning and application. By engaging in real-world projects that address the pressing issues in their communities, participants can immediately put their newfound knowledge into practice.

Fostering a supportive network among participants encourages the exchange of experiences and insights, creating a thriving community of learners. Moreover, the training should not exist in isolation; it must evolve and adapt over time. Continuous monitoring and evaluation are crucial for assessing the effectiveness of these programs. Gathering feedback from participants ensures that improvements are made where necessary, making the training truly responsive to the needs of grassroots workers.

In addition to building skills, these programs should also promote advocacy for open data initiatives. Participants should be empowered to champion the cause within their communities and learn how to effectively engage with local stakeholders and potential donors. Moreover, forging partnerships with local institutions and organizations ensures the sustainability of these initiatives, creating a robust ecosystem of support for grassroots NGO workers. By following these steps, we enable these individuals to harness the power of open data as a force for positive change in their economically disadvantaged areas.

Here is a cheat sheet aimed at total beginners to open data; you can either create your own version and print it as a handout or use it as a basis to create a training session, but don't forget that at the end of the book you will find a full workshop manuscript you can use:

UNLOCKING THE POWER OF OPEN DATA: A NEIGHBORHOOD GUIDE

WHAT'S THE BUZZ ABOUT OPEN DATA?

Ever wondered how you can learn more about your neighborhood, the projects happening around you, or maybe even some cool local facts? Well, that's where open data comes in. It's like a treasure trove of information that's free for all of us to explore and use.

WHY SHOULD YOU CARE?

Discover Your Community: Open data helps you uncover what's really going on in your area. From new construction projects to local events, it's all there.

Become a Problem Solver: Got an idea to make your neighborhood even better? Open data can be your secret weapon for finding solutions.

Connect with Neighbors: Want to chat with others about what's happening around you? Open data is a conversation starter that can bring your community closer together.

WHERE TO FIND OPEN DATA

Local Websites: Your city council or community groups often share open data on their websites. It's like a local information hub.

Talk to Your People: Don't be shy—reach out to your neighbors, community leaders, or tech-savvy friends. They might know where to dig up valuable data.

Online Tools: The internet is a goldmine of information. Websites such as data. gov offer data from all over. You can search for data related to your area.

GETTING SMART WITH OPEN DATA

Check the Rules: Some data sets have rules about how you can use them. Always follow the guidelines and give credit where it's due.

Spread the Love: When you use data, don't forget to thank the folks who shared it. It's a small gesture that goes a long way.

Stay Current: Make sure you're using the latest data. Things change fast, and you want your information to be up-to-date.

TOOLS OF THE TRADE

Basic Spreadsheets: You don't need to be a data wizard. Simple tools such as Excel or Google Sheets can help you work with data.

Visualize Your Insights: Turn boring numbers into exciting charts and graphs. It's like painting a picture with data.

Ask for a Hand: If you get stuck, reach out to a neighbor or a friend who knows their way around data. Teamwork makes the dream work.

JOIN THE OPEN DATA CLUB

Meet Locals: Look for or start local groups that discuss open data. It's a great way to connect with like-minded folks from your area.

Online Communities: Explore online forums where open data enthusiasts hang out. You can swap stories and ideas, and maybe even collaborate on exciting projects.

Give Back: If you have skills to share, consider lending a hand on open data initiatives or volunteering for data-related tasks in your community.

In a nutshell, open data isn't just for tech gurus or data scientists—it's for you, your neighbors, and everyone in your community. So, dive in, explore, and unlock the potential of open data to make your neighborhood shine brighter than ever!

We as citizens understand the digital divide in our communities better than anybody else, better than your local representatives, and better than any report, because it's our home and the citizens around us are our people.

Building a community network is an integral component of addressing the digital divide collectively. In our modern, interconnected world, merely imparting digital skills to individuals isn't sufficient. We must also foster an environment that nurtures their growth and encourages mutual support.

Shared Learning Spaces: These spaces, whether physical locations or virtual platforms, serve as hubs where individuals gather to exchange knowledge. They can take various forms, ranging from community centers and online forums to regular meetups. In these settings, participants engage in discussions, address challenges, share valuable insights, and draw from each other's experiences. It is within these Shared Learning Spaces that the true potential of collective learning and collaborative problem-solving comes to life.

Mentorship Programs: Establishing mentorship programs within the community network can be immensely valuable. Experienced individuals can guide newcomers, offering advice, encouragement, and practical solutions to digital challenges. Such programs foster a sense of belonging and provide a safety net for those navigating the digital world for the first time.

Collaborative Projects: Encouraging collaborative projects is another way to promote mutual support. When participants join forces on projects that address local issues, they not only apply their newly acquired digital skills but also strengthen their sense of community. These projects could range from creating community websites to developing data-driven solutions for local challenges.

Resource Sharing: In a supportive network, resource sharing is key. Participants can pool their resources, such as access to technology, internet connectivity, or even relevant data sources. This sharing ensures that everyone has equitable access to the tools and information needed to bridge the digital gap.

Advocacy and Awareness: Collectively advocating for digital inclusion is essential. The community network can work together to raise awareness about the digital divide, engage with local policymakers and institutions, and lobby for affordable internet access and digital literacy programs. By amplifying their voices as a collective, participants can drive meaningful change in their communities.

In essence, fostering a supportive community network is about recognizing that the digital divide cannot be bridged in isolation. It requires individuals to come together, sharing their strengths, and collectively working towards digital equity. Through these collaborative efforts, we can ensure that no one is left behind in our increasingly digital world.

Addressing the digital divide starts at home, and it is as important as physical community development. Open data can help us paint the picture, set out the need, and target what we would like to change, but also measure that impact.

Taking a community-driven and collaborative approach, we can create a baseline that is unique to you, your area, and its actors. If you don't, it won't work—there is no one-size-fits-all solution, and just copying procedures from other areas won't suffice. You and your colleagues are just as unique as the places you support. Don't forget that.

NOTES

1 Eriksen, Thomas Hylland. (2020). "Filling the apps: The smartphone, time and the refugee." *Waiting and the Temporalities of Irregular Migration*. Routledge, 57–72.
2 "Pay the Wi-Fi or Feed the Children: Coronavirus Has Intensified the UK's Digital Divide." Cambridge University. https://www.cam.ac.uk/stories/digitaldivide
3 UNICEF. (2020, November 30). Two-Thirds of the World's School-Age Children Have No Internet Access at Home. https://www.unicef.org/press-releases/two-thirds-worlds-school-age-children-have-no-internet-access-home-new-unicef-itu#:~:text=NEW%20YORK%2FGENEVA%2C%201%20December,International%20Telecommunication%20Union%20(ITU)
4 Brennan, M. (2017, June 29). Black Country Victim of 'Digital Divide' with UK's Lowest Rates of Internet Use. *Express & Star*. https://www.expressandstar.com/news/2017/06/29/black-country-victim-of-digital-divide-with-uks-lowest-rates-of-internet-use/

Open Doors, Open Data

4

Making Your Data "Open" and Licensing

If you have data, why should you consider making it open? Let's explore.

To most people, including some technologists, the idea of creating and releasing open data can be a mind-blowing concept. But, it's not as complicated as it may seem. It can be pretty straightforward. If you come from the not-for-profit sector, I encourage you all to consider these steps as they demonstrate your openness to collaboration, having a free and open society, and your active commitment to it.

But why should you bother to release data? Apart from showing that your organization cares about community cohesion, it can serve as a fantastic marketing tool. Grant-giving entities appreciate organizations that are committed to openness,[1] and it also encourages other organizations to collaborate with you (Figure 4.1).

If you have information that you would like to release as open data, you must first ensure that you comply with all the legal, ethical, and other requirements outlined in your institution's privacy policy and the common law of the country you reside in.

You must also acknowledge the contributions of individuals outside your organization, such as researchers or collaborators. Any external data should be attributed to its source, and you should adhere to its terms and conditions,[2] if applicable.

Common and legal advice is as follows[3]:

- Ensure the data you have is in accordance with the best practices of your organization.
- You must make sure the data is open to anyone without any restrictions.
- Make sure the data can be built upon and reused.
- Make sure any information that could identify somebody, such as name, postcode, and date of birth, is removed from the dataset.

DOI: 10.1201/9781032724645-4

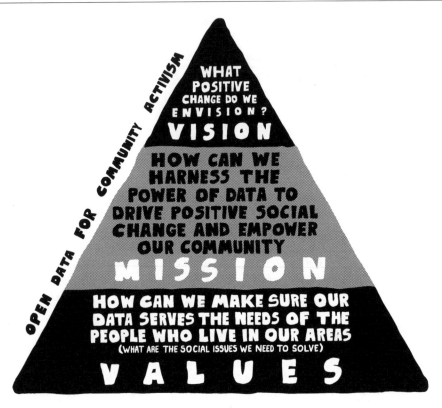

FIGURE 4.1 What are the vision, mission, and values we should consider when making our data open?

Let's explore what you will have to think about when creating your dataset[4]:

1. **Completeness:** you will need to make sure the dataset is as finished as possible and does not have unfinished areas or gaps. If the data is raw, make sure you add metadata explaining what the data is, along with any formulas to calculate the data. This is important, as it will help users get a clear grasp of what you are releasing.
2. **Primary Sources:** make sure you have quoted all of the sources and explain how you collected all of the data.
3. **Proximity in Time:** make sure your data is available for a decent period and updated, especially if the data will change with time or from day to day—this is a little more advanced and may not apply. This is the amount of data an app would use, like a train timetable, website for example.
4. **Easy to Access:** make sure your dataset is as accessible as possible; this means it should be easy to view and open to everybody, which means do not use paid software native files, and if you can, try to ensure it can be opened by open-source software.

5. **Ensure Your Data Is Machine Readable:** if you have handwritten notes, perhaps from surveys or notes from workshop activities, you will need to ensure this is typed up so your computer can access it; never release handwritten documents as data; it is not accessible to everybody—to help you here, you can use Optical Character Recognition (OCR) software, which will process this for you on the most part, but you will have to clean this up as it may not be able to recognize the text; there is free and open-source software that can help you do this.
6. **Non-Discrimination:** make sure your dataset can be downloaded and then opened on easy-to-access or free software.
7. **Use Open Standards:** when you save your dataset, make sure that the file can be opened by any program and not a program that would cost someone money to use.
8. **Licensing:** for the data to be called "open data," you will need to license it as such; there are loads of different open license mechanisms out there that are easy to use and which you can access with little or no legal know-how.

Finally, let's examine the checklist for releasing your open data:

- Select the dataset you intend to make open, ensuring that identities are removed and keeping the process simple without unnecessary complications.
- Apply an open license to your dataset.
- Publish your data. Many government institutions use ckan.org, an open-source data management tool designed for storing and distributing open data.
- Promote your data by sharing it on the web and organizing a central catalog on your website to showcase the data.

With all these points considered, you may now be considering the data you have that could be released. However, to truly classify it as open data,[5] and I am saying this again as I want to hammer it home, it needs to be licensed accordingly. Although it may seem like an unnecessary step, it's important to remember that you own the data and you want people to acknowledge the source, making a license not only a legal protection but also a means of promotion.

Having a license in place also simplifies your life. For instance, if someone wants to use your data or any other work, such as a photograph, they would typically need to seek your permission. By licensing your work, you remove the need for individual requests, as the chosen license will outline the permissions and conditions for use.

In simpler terms, it's a way to copyright your work while still enabling anyone to access, modify, or use it as they wish, as long as they give you credit. Again, it is recommended to use a Creative Commons license, as all the legal aspects have already been taken care of.

Before we move on, let's explore what you have to your advantage. There are two specific open licenses I want to turn your attention to: Creative Commons[6] and Open Data Commons.[7]

Creative Commons licenses offer small, third-sector organizations an accessible and adaptable method for sharing creative works and data, even without extensive technical expertise. Their user-friendly nature, customization options, and the support of a large community make them an ideal choice for newcomers to data sharing. However, it's essential to note that these licenses might lack the data-specific clarity and precision offered by Open Data Commons licenses.

Open Data Commons, which is an open license developed by the Open Knowledge Foundation, is a license that caters specifically to data sharing, providing explicit terms and conditions that reduce ambiguity and potential legal risks for organizations with limited legal knowledge. These licenses align with open data principles and can be an advantageous choice for organizations focusing on data-sharing initiatives.

Mario Wiedemann from the Bertelsmann Stiftung leads the "Data for Society" (Daten für die Gesellschaft) project, someone I've had the opportunity to work closely with. Together, we designed a training toolkit for the country, aiming to make open data more understandable and foster relationships between local government and the third sector. He emphasizes the untapped potential of civil society organizations: "Civil society organizations do a lot of good in various ways. In Germany, they haven't been as active in sharing open data compared to government offices. But here's the thing: these organizations have loads of valuable data, too. Their data can be used to expand the overall data available to everyone. Sometimes, these groups have unique information that nobody else has. Sharing this fills in the gaps in data and helps build a complete picture of important social topics."

Wiedemann suggests that civil society take a test-and-learn approach: "For smaller organizations, sharing data openly might be a bit tough at first. One way to start is by using data already available in publications or on their website, even if it doesn't meet the open data standards yet. This helps them learn how to turn their information into open data. And for any organization planning to regularly share open data, they should assign someone responsible for overseeing this. In larger organizations, it's not just one person's job; everyone should be involved. While having experts to contact is vital, it's also crucial to train everyone to handle data well. This way, the whole organization is ready to work with data effectively."

In the rest of the book, we will get to grips with the real nitty-gritty of releasing and, of course, using open data. We'll talk about privacy, sovereignty, misinformation, practical platforms to put your data out there using open source, why you should collect community-driven data, and much more. Ready? Let's continue our journey.

NOTES

1 Carman, J. G. (2009). Nonprofits, funders, and evaluation: Accountability in action. *The American Review of Public Administration*, 39(4), 374–390. https://doi.org/10.1177/0275074008320190
2 Murray-Rust, P. (2008). Open data in science. *Nature Precedings*. https://www.nature.com/nature

3 Welle Donker, F., & van Loenen, B. (2016). How to assess the success of the open data ecosystem? *Journal of Spatial Information Science*, 10, 284–306. https://doi.org/10.1080/1 7538947.2016.1224938

4 European Commission, Charlotte van Ooijen, David Osimo, David Regeczi, Elena Simperl, Eline Lincklaen Arriëns, Hidde Holl, Jochem Dogger, Laura van Knippenberg, Myrte ter Horst, Oscar Corcho, & Sofie Finn Storan. (2023). *Rethinking Impact of Open Data*. ISBN 978-92-78-43399-4.

5 Murray-Rust, P. (2008). Open data in science. *Nature Precedings*. https://doi.org/10.1038/npre.2008.1526.1

6 Creative Commons. (n.d.). Licenses. https://creativecommons.org/licenses/list.en

7 Open Data Commons. (n.d.). Home. https://opendatacommons.org/

Making Open Data Outreach Human-Centered

5

Human-centered design strives to start by comprehending the specific needs of the individuals you're designing for and ultimately deliver innovative solutions that precisely address those needs at their core. The primary goal of human-centered design is to cultivate a profound sense of empathy for the target audience. This involves generating a list of concepts, creating prototypes, sharing your work with the target audience, and involving them in the subsequent steps.

In simple terms, creating a new product or service becomes a collaborative endeavor. The genuine requirements of users take center stage, and a specific problem is approached from their perspective, iterating through multiple feedback loops to address that need. In contrast to traditional product development, human-centered design engages the user throughout the entire process, not merely at the end.

A vital component of human-centered design involves the development of open data programs tailored to the needs of specific user groups. By comprehending the varied interests of different users, a city can improve the accessibility and utility of open data, ultimately empowering its citizens to make more informed decisions (Figure 5.1).

Let me provide you with a personal example to illustrate how this works in practice.

In 2017, I was approached by the Sandwell Metropolitan Borough Council, a local government body in the West Midlands region of England, to design a smart city project in the area. When I heard the term "smart city," I immediately understood their expectations. However, I declined their offer, which surprised them.

Smaller governments often envision smart city projects in larger cities as utopian concepts of digitalization. But what does it really mean?

A smart city is a municipality that leverages information and communication technology (ICT) to enhance administrative efficiency, disseminate information to the public, and improve public services and the well-being of residents.

Although the term "smart city" has gained popularity among senior government officials, it remains vague and undefined. Currently, it encompasses a wide range of projects and concepts related to urban development.

DOI: 10.1201/9781032724645-5

RESEACH THE NEEDS, CHALLENGES AND GOALS
OF COMMUNITY PROJECTS TO ENSURE YOUR DATA IS RELEVANT.

DETERMINE HOW YOU WANT THE DATA TO BE USED. WHETHER FOR COLLABORATION ISSUE HIGHLIGHTING AND SOCIAL ACTION.

WHAT MAKES SENSE TO THE LOCAL COMMUNITY IN REGARDS TO FORMAT. DESIGN AND USAGE.

1 UDERSTAND YOUR AUDIENCE

2 DEFINE CLEAR OBJECTIVES

3 ASK AROUND

4 ENSURE ACCESSIBILITY AND USER-FRIENDLY DESIGN

5 CONTINUOUS FEEDBACK AND ADJUSTMENT

HUMAN CENTERED DESIGN AND OPEN DATA

CONTINUOUSLY GATHER INPUT, AND ADAPT YOUR OPEN DATA INITIATIVES BASED ON USER FEEDBACK AND EVOLVING NEEDS

PRESENT YOUR OPEN DATA IN A USER-FRIENDLY WAY. CONSIDER HOW YOU HOST IT (E.G. YOUR WEBSITE, VIA A BLOG. OR OPEN SOURCE PLATFORMS.

FIGURE 5.1 The steps to consider to make your open data human-centered.

A smart city is a technologically driven urban infrastructure that encompasses environmental initiatives, an efficient public transportation system, effective urban planning, and the facilitation of living, working, and utilizing the city's resources. Its aim is to enhance the city's appeal to residents and businesses by improving and expanding city services.

For a smart city to truly succeed in its traditional sense, it requires a robust ecosystem of academic institutions, healthcare facilities, corporate entities, and transportation infrastructure surrounding the city authority. These entities are typically involved in the design process through various activities such as steering groups, market halls, corporate meetups, hackathons, and workshops.

However, in poorer areas, universities may be lacking, healthcare systems may be underfunded and overburdened, and essential facilities like train stations may be absent. Take Dudley, for instance, the second-largest town in the UK, with a population larger than many major European cities, yet it only has a bus station.

Nevertheless, these areas are encouraged to implement their own smart city projects, often due to pressure from the central government. However, due to a lack of education and training, they tend to emulate what larger cities are doing, which may not be suitable for their specific context and ultimately lead to failure.

This is what I expected when Sandwell Metropolitan Council approached me, so I recommended that they consider an alternative route.

To move forward with the project, we decided to take a different approach—a human-centered approach. I made it clear that the project would not proceed unless significant efforts were made to improve community infrastructure, address skills gaps, and fulfill digital needs. I believed that ignoring these aspects would alienate the community organizations that form the social fabric of the area, as they would feel we were just force-feeding them the new usual buzzwords.

I positioned the project as a community-centric smart city platform and implemented mechanisms that allowed attendees at events to co-design the project or at least have a say in its direction. This approach gained considerable traction. We engaged with the communities, designing the project with their input and offering training.

To give you some context, West Bromwich, the largest and most well-known of the six towns that make up Sandwell, is an extremely industrial area. Report after report consistently ranks it among the top ten most impoverished areas in the UK. There are 186 Lower Super Output Areas (LSOAs) in Sandwell out of the 32,844 LSOAs in England.[1] In 2019, one in five of Sandwell's LSOAs were located in the nation's 10% most deprived areas. Overall, 60% of Sandwell's LSOAs fall within the worst 20% nationally and 97% within the worst 60% nationally, showing the severe levels of deprivation that are present in many areas of the county. An additional two-fifths fall among the most impoverished 10%–20%.

My job required me to connect frequently with the public; I had to come up with a strategy to gather data to support a policy and evidence of how we worked with community organizations to advance the project. I designed a few participatory activities for each workshop to collect qualitative data because I knew that anything corporate simply wouldn't stick and that it would be a constant battle to engage people. I used general digital training as a medium to get people to attend these events (Figure 5.2).

USING OPEN DATA TO ADDRESS HYPERLOCAL DIGITAL SKILLS GAPS

LOCAL DATA COLLECTION
GATHER DATA SPECIFIC TO YOUR NEIGHBORHOOD'S DIGITAL SKILLS GAPS

CUSTOMIZED TRAINING

COMMUNITY ENGAGEMENT
INVOLVE COMMUNITY IN DATA COLLECTION AND ADDRESS NEEDS

LOCAL DATA SOURCES
UTILISE OPEN DATA RELATED TO YOUR AREA TO ENHANCE TRAINING MATERIALS

MEASURING IMPACT
TRACK AND ANALYSE HOW OPEN DATA-DRIVEN TRAINING IS IMPROVING DIGITAL SKILLS LOCALLY

FIGURE 5.2   Local open data can serve as a foundation for designing customized training programs that tackle specific digital skill gaps in diverse areas. Data isn't limited to traditional forms; it offers flexibility. If you can't find the necessary data, consider collecting your own through surveys. This self-collected data can effectively steer and propel your initiatives; here is how.

We would demonstrate, almost gently, through these events how they could uti-lize open data to enhance their personnel and services, but after some NGO employees attended a few sessions, open data lacked that corporate identity. Why? We made sure that the first time they heard about it, it was in a relevant setting and not what many of these initiatives saw as corporate language. It is easy; because of its image, they would have never thought to seek it out or blink twice if you had mentioned it to them before.

You see, putting the needs of the human being at the center of your design need not be obvious; it may also be a thought process.

And that method is capable of developing its own ecosystems. NGOs in one of the most impoverished regions of England were utilizing Sandwell Council's open data for funding applications and reports with what seemed like no effort at all, and they were truly pleased about it. It demonstrated to me that third-sector employees, even volun-teers, could comprehend the idea of what may be considered to be something extremely technical, such as open data, and that the outreach narratives presented earlier were what prevented some third-sector employees from locating or using it.

This revealed to me that, really, it's not a big deal to involve the third sector in this, and if this approach could work in an area like Sandwell, which has some of the weak-est education outcomes in the country as outlined in the UK Government Department for Education's white paper in 2022,[2] high levels of poverty,[3] and a dense population, it could work anywhere, with a little thought.

Open data has its image crisis due to government agencies wanting corporations and academic institutions to use it and not really seeing the value of the third sector accessing their platforms, so they customized the aesthetics accordingly, and it stayed. It's simple marketing and understanding your target; there is no secret science behind it. This is precisely how open data acquired its strong corporate appearance in the first place.

In this case, effective marketing simply involves leveraging local knowledge, understanding community needs, and using language that will elicit favorable reactions from the target audience.

Over the period of the project, we ran various training campaigns ranging from social media to capacity building, fitting in as many opportunities as we could to gather evidence to drive the Council's inclusive digitization agenda with a basis of honest com-munity consultation from those who work in grassroots organizations.

The main objective of a smart city is to develop an urban setting that offers its citizens a good quality of life while simultaneously fostering general economic growth. Having a culture where people use open data for social good is essential, in my opin-ion, and making effective use of all things digital is crucial to fostering community resilience.

I personally believe you can't do that without really getting to know the needs of citizens and the organizations that support them. This is what happens in Sandwell now: various steering groups and community projects craft the region's digital decision-mak-ing process.

Along with "human-centered" in the context of design and product development, the term "design thinking" is also frequently used, primarily in the private sector.

With design thinking, the emphasis is on the users' actual needs, and to meet those demands, many feedback loops are used to examine a given problem from the users' perspective. The user is involved throughout the entire process, not just at the conclusion, which sets it apart from typical product development.

In their research and development efforts, many businesses employ design thinking. But over the past few years, Design Thinking has also grown in popularity in the public sector; a number of Innovation Labs have been established recently in order to use the Design Thinking principles in the public sector to develop solutions that are centered on the needs of the citizens. Examples include the Mohammed Bin Rashid Centre for Government Innovation in the United Arab Emirates, which assists government organizations in their innovation efforts, and the Digital Transformation Agency in Australia, which develops online services in collaboration with and for the benefit of public administrations.

This is where the lines get blurred a little bit because of this corporate-minded design-thinking influence from innovative government departments. This has a knock-on effect as now large innovative third-sector organizations seek out corporately trained professionals to join their teams to mirror their counterparts.

For the record, this method brings some incredible and talented individuals to the third sector, but every action has a reaction, and in reality, this approach draws individuals with a commercial emphasis. After all, it's about money, isn't it? Not so much generating it but also streamlining services to work better. You can brand it however you like, but it all comes down to making things work better for less.

It's really simple: product designers are driven to create sales for businesses, and that is the background the majority of these people come from. The clue is in the name of the job title; they are trained to design products to send out to market; if the product is not marketable, it will fail; and how would they measure if the product is marketable or not? Either how much it has made or how much money it has saved in a governmental sense.

We need to come full circle and really consider just how human-centered our systems design thinking really is; regardless of the outreach rhetoric, all you need to look at is how government and larger third sectors recruit, go and look at some strategy design-type job openings, and look at the language. Do they sound inclusive, and do you feel these types of professionals can connect with, let alone understand, the needs of grassroots organizations?

Acceptance is important as it is linked to trust. Citizens are more likely to accept changes if their needs and ideas are taken into account while creating new products and services to address societal issues.

Finally, human-centered steps to consider when approaching open data outreach projects or strategies aimed at encouraging third-sector organizations to use it for social good are:

1. **Better Understand Your Audience:** Use need-finding techniques, such as interviews, open days, workshops, or simply engaging with the community and reaching out to civil society organizations. This helps you comprehend the policy challenge in both breadth and depth and gather insights that aid in articulating a shared vision for the new policy with a genuine impact on residents.

2. **Define Your Goals:** Determine your desired outcomes based on the vision. Once you have a clear vision, gather your team and analyze examples of best practices that have already proven successful in achieving similar objectives elsewhere. Look for examples that you admire and would like to emulate.

3. **Analyze Your Findings:** Comprehend the research thoroughly and compare the desired results to identify the best approach for achieving the pre-established objectives.

4. **Engage Senior Leadership or Policymakers:** Present the potential mechanism after choosing the best model and seek input from your leadership. Involving senior leadership is crucial before proceeding to outreach with important stakeholders, as it helps identify necessary changes that align with the organization-wide policy.

5. **Test and Learn:** Exercise creativity in this phase. For example, if you are developing a strategy to persuade regional grassroots organizations to use open data from a specific data bank or website, invite a small cohort from one sector (e.g., environmental groups) to attend your outreach events and utilize the data. Collect qualitative and quantitative information, such as through surveys and interviews, over a predetermined time period.

6. **Evaluate Progress:** Review all your findings, including the original goals, the vision from your leadership or policymakers, feedback, and the results of your test-and-learn activities. Identify any gaps that arise, and use this opportunity to pause, listen, learn, and adapt.

7. **Deploy:** Once you have gone through the evaluation stage, you are ready to launch your project. Continuously use the test-and-learn approach by conducting surveys, interviews, and regular workshops. Incorporate your efforts into training sessions, including adding open data components to existing training from other sources. Encourage colleagues and other service providers to include a section in their work that describes how to access and utilize your data.

By adopting a human-centered design approach, it becomes easier for civil society organizations to access and use open data, empowering them to participate in public debate and accountability more efficiently. City governments can build trust with specific user groups and communities by designing for their needs, thus encouraging civic action for the greater good. Even activists who are not part of the government or any organization that releases open data can apply this style of thinking to hold people accountable or create campaigns that promote openness using human-centered design methods.

NOTES

1   Sandwell Metropolitan Borough Council. (2023). Deprivation - West Midlands Context. https://www.sandwelltrends.info/deprivation_west_midlands_context/#:~:text=England% 20is%20made%20up%20of,deprived%2010%25%20nationally%20in%202019

2 Department for Education. (2022, March 28). Opportunity for All: Strong Schools with Great Teachers for Your Child. https://www.gov.uk/government/publications/opportunity-for-all-strong-schools-with-great-teachers-for-your-child

3 Public Health Department, Sandwell Metropolitan Borough Council. (2017). Joint Strategic Needs Assessment (JSNA) for Children and Young People Aged 5–19 Years Old. https://www.sandwelltrends.info/wp-content/uploads/sites/5/2018/06/JSNA_CYP-5to19-years-2017.pdf

The Language around Open Data and Adding Public Value to Our Narrative

6

I don't know what it is with open data. Regarding outreach, why do we talk about it as if it's quantum physics?

You could argue that open data has an unjust reputation. The question is, does it deserve it? The answer is yes and no. Open data is often associated with a corporate image shaped by the sector that has adopted it. Consequently, the image and, more significantly, the language used heavily reflect that influence. However, it's not open data's fault.

This medium specifically focuses on a neglected group when it comes to inclusion: the third sector. I'm not solely addressing tech-savvy NGOs; I'm also acknowledging the invaluable contributions of grassroots organizations that genuinely impact individuals' lives.

For close to a decade, activism has been a prominent aspect of my life, predating my involvement in policy design. One tool I've consistently championed is the utilization of digital platforms to ensure accountability among our policymakers and hold them to their commitments.

In all sincerity, I firmly believe that this is where the authentic potential of open data lies—as a catalyst for driving social change and authentically shaping policies and strategic trajectories.

Open data has the potential to empower NGOs and catalyze social change by providing them with valuable insights and advocacy tools. By accessing and analyzing open data, NGOs can gather evidence to support their causes, identify patterns, and comprehend the impact of social issues. Open data allows NGOs to highlight disparities, inequalities, and areas in need of improvement, which can inform their advocacy efforts and drive policy change. Furthermore, it's important to recognize that NGOs possess a unique opportunity for fruitful collaboration with other organizations. They can come together to share best practices, align their efforts towards common objectives, and

DOI: 10.1201/9781032724645-6

harness the potential of open data to amplify their impact. This collaborative approach not only enhances their effectiveness but also fosters meaningful engagement with stakeholders, ultimately driving positive social change in our communities.

However, a significant hurdle lies in the fact that many of these organizations remain unaware of the immense possibilities that open data offers. It's understandable, as they are not the primary target audience for open data initiatives.

When you explore various open data portals worldwide, you might find them intriguing. These portals often present themselves with designs and language that could easily be mistaken for corporate entities in their own right. If you have used open data before, honestly think about it. Recall the places where you've obtained data in the past—how business-focused did they seem?

I'm not saying it's a bad thing or that they shouldn't look that way. It's the foundation of many scientific and academic projects. Open data is regularly used by the healthcare, academic, and corporate sectors, which play a crucial role in our civic systems. These areas provide jobs, research, and vital infrastructure for our cities and towns.

However, I strongly believe we can do more to help grassroots organizations in our community use data. In my experience, a complete redesign isn't needed just yet. Instead, we require a more holistic approach through community development and campaigns.

The biggest barrier to engaging our NGOs isn't the technicalities of open data, where to find it, or even how to implement it into their work. Because, well, it doesn't have to be any of those things if it's explained clearly and in an easily understandable manner.

The answer lies in language.

A skilled community developer will tell you that you need to find common ground with the people you're trying to engage with. Open data is a challenging subject to relate to, especially for non-academics, corporate executives, and technocrats. But there are other ways for people to take the initiative and seek it out. You just need to paint a picture that is closer to your target audience.

I use storytelling as a means to translate open data stipulations, analyses, or activities into layman's terms. It provides a hook to generate interest and can be integrated into a community's involvement in the issue. Trust me, if you plan to explain open data practices to your local third sector, the narrative is your most important tool. Especially if you're operating in an area with job scarcity, deprivation, and a limited tech industry, taking that approach is essential.

From London to Seoul and New York, open data is at the core of the digital agenda to enhance the city's ecosystem, foster connections with professionals, and generate ideas to address city-level issues, spanning from healthcare and education to democracy. It possesses the power to transform social, economic, and environmental landscapes and contribute to more effective governance.

But what about places such as Dudley, Chemnitz, and Ramallah? These smaller towns and cities may not have the technological infrastructure or academic prestige that larger urban centers boast. The question I often ponder is: should we abandon the residents of these places, pushing them to leave their homes in search of opportunities in our bigger cities? The resounding answer is no, of course, and I'm sure we all share this sentiment.

To create a thriving environment for innovation that involves the third sector, businesses, educational institutions, government entities, and activists, we must take specific measures to be as inclusive in our decision-making as possible.

I've had various successes in setting up community-oriented projects to facilitate conversations around digital engagement, such as pop-up coworking spaces, accelerator programs, and microfunds for community projects. It is important to be aware that data can serve as the linchpin connecting citizens and organizations. But the challenge lies in finding a way to bring them together, and language plays a pivotal role in this endeavor. Think of it as effective marketing—the right narrative can attract people and encourage active participation.

Regardless of the political stance of your government—whether it leans left, right, or center—populism often plays a significant role. This presents an opportunity for advocacy. In this populist context,[1] "the people" are seen as champions of the greater good, while "the elite" are portrayed as self-serving and corrupt. The former group vastly outnumbers the latter. Consequently, when a substantial number of people or a movement voice their concerns, it becomes politically advantageous for officials to demonstrate responsiveness and show they are listening—because that's votes, people.

If decision-makers witness a successful outreach model, they may be influenced to do more. However, in my view, waiting for elected officials doesn't accomplish much. You need to ask the question and take it upon yourself to be a public disruptor. If you can gather enough traction, they will follow suit, albeit under some pressure.

Disruptive innovation, a concept pioneered by Clayton Christensen,[2] describes the emergence of new, often simpler, and more affordable technologies or solutions that gradually replace established products or services in the market. Christensen's theory underscores how this process can bring about substantial transformations within industries.

For community activists aiming to wield influence with digital policy, embracing the principles of disruptive innovation entails recognizing that change can arise unexpectedly. By remaining vigilant about accessible technologies and advocating for policies that promote innovation and healthy competition, activists can play a vital role in ensuring that underserved communities can access the benefits of emerging digital opportunities. This approach urges policymakers to adopt regulations and strategies in response to disruptive developments, thereby contributing to the development of a digital landscape that is more inclusive and equitable for all.

It may sound somewhat absurd to claim that we need radical change to make something unnecessarily complex like open data relatable again. But unless we take community-friendly outreach seriously, charities, voluntary organizations, and civil society will genuinely miss out on a tool that can help them improve the effectiveness and seamlessness of their operations, and that gap will just get bigger.

Imagine yourself as a volunteer on the business development team of a food bank situated in your local area. What would make your job much easier? Would it be access to local data on households with low incomes, deprivation scores from nearby neighborhoods, the number of support grants provided by local governments to homes, or even the count of budget supermarkets in the area? Do you believe this type of data could assist you in crafting engagement strategies, project models, or grant applications?

The answer should be yes, but if you haven't been trained or engaged in a way to understand why these statistics would benefit your cause, there's no way you would actively seek out that information.

When evaluating policy outreach, regardless of the issue, I frequently place myself in scenarios such as this. I find it helps me design more engaging projects.

Taking this mindset means I have to fine-tune our outreach model, as it allows us to understand what resonates with grassroots organizations in high-deprivation areas when it comes to encouraging them to utilize, seek out, or request data. Therefore, I would like to share with you some of the key themes that attracted third-sector and voluntary participants to training or hackathons, which are rapid prototyping workshops that focus on gathering intelligence through participative activities over a short amount of time.

It's fair to say that these themes may seem obvious, but sometimes stating the obvious is exactly what is needed. We will cover these topics a fair bit throughout the book.

FUNDING

Considering the next chapter primarily focuses on this topic, I will delve into its importance later in the book. However, for explanatory purposes, it is crucial to highlight that using open data as evidence for funding tenders or grant applications was highly appealing to participants.

REPORTING, MAPPING, AND MONITORING SOCIAL TRENDS

Enabling the third sector to recognize the value of utilizing data changes to demonstrate the impact of their work and reinforce evidence of their community contribution is always advantageous. Open data serves as a foundation for factual reports that effectively illustrate the organization's significance in the area.

Campaigning, Blogging, and Journalism

Incorporating open data into blogging can enhance transparency, strengthen advocacy initiatives, and provide evidence-based insights to drive positive social change.

The key lies in effectively communicating with third-sector workers and presenting the information in a relatable manner during training sessions. We have discovered that when they understand how open data can be utilized and visualized in their work, they actively seek out and request it, provided there is accessible support and clear guidance.

Now, let's explore the impact of language on both local government and the third sector in terms of digitalization.

Based on a series of workshops that I personally conducted with government and third-sector workers worldwide, these were the common themes collected from the questionnaires:

GOVERNMENT OFFICERS

While it is true that many employees have a solid grasp of open data, a significant number of them find themselves hesitating to seek clarification or raise questions due to a self-imposed expectation that they need to be the experts, especially senior staff or heads of department. This can result in miscommunication of strategy and muddies the waters with outreach, as sometimes it is an interpretation of what they perceive open data to be or the difference it can make. Nurturing an environment where questions are encouraged, knowledge is shared, and continuous learning is valued would not only streamline the narrative but also foster a culture of empowerment and collaboration within the organization.

The presence of siloed work within the government further hampers the ability of workers to develop cohesive outreach plans. The fragmented nature of collaboration makes it difficult to coordinate efforts effectively.

CHARITY, COMMUNITY, AND VOLUNTARY STAFF

The majority of staff members felt that they struggled to grasp the concept of open data due to the language surrounding it, which seemed too corporate and unfamiliar to them. Mixing this with trust issues between the third sector and local government, they felt a lot of the digital narrative was just jargon, and they have often dismissed digital outreach as nonsense and ignored government outreach entirely on this issue.

Where does "public value" come into this debate? Let us explore this.

I know it may seem unusual to juxtapose public value and digital policy, but in this context, particularly considering how open data can benefit neighborhood-level organizations, it is important to incorporate this type of thinking when formulating open data outreach strategies.

To achieve that, we must analyze how "public value" integrates into our work as staff members or activists. We need to consider how it resonates with the people in our communities and outline the desired outcomes for our towns and cities.

Policymakers play a crucial role in determining how to utilize the powers of the state by collectively envisioning a good and just society. As public servants or policymakers, it is their responsibility to help citizens articulate their goals and needs and then use their positions to put them into practice.

Creating a framework that empowers citizens to influence decisions and promote meaningful engagement is essential. Involving NGOs or grassroots community organizations from the outset allows them to shape the agenda and policy narrative, which is what they desire based on my experience in community activism.

If you are a public servant, elected official, policymaker, or anyone involved in impacting people's lives, your duty is to create public value.[3] You need to look beyond policies and procedures and continuously question whether you are utilizing all available resources to enhance the prosperity, civility, and fairness of society.

To accomplish this, we must embrace innovative thinking, creativity, and inventiveness to foster a mindset that generates greater value.

The term "value" often carries a transactional connotation. It can help us explain certain services effectively. For example, it appeals to many individuals as a means to hold governments accountable for their performance. People scrutinize their respective governments' budget days, passing judgment on issues like the potential lack of investment in healthcare or taxes affecting the price of goods.

Another perspective is evaluating government performance by envisioning concrete and objectively valuable outcomes resulting from decisions or policies. This provides decision-makers with a practical way to assess the positive impact generated by their choices.

Understanding these transactional perspectives is crucial for grassroots third-sector workers collaborating with local governments. It can help establish rapport and effective communication with public sector colleagues.

In my work with grant-giving organizations, I have observed that the funder's standpoint places significant importance on the level of engagement outlined in funding tenders and the value that these engagements ultimately deliver.

However, we must also consider the moral dimensions of "value." It encompasses aspirations and the sense of meaning it brings to life—a vision of a good and just society.

Returning to the discussion of data and outreach, articulating the public value of open data is vital. Whether as an NGO worker aiming to collect data for social good or any other stakeholder, explaining the impact of open data and helping others visualize the social change it can bring is crucial. Open data as a movement should emphasize collective participation and decision-making, reflecting the inclusive "we" rather than the individual "I."

To effectively communicate with different groups, we must present open data and capacity-building tools in a way that resonates with them. Creating cohesive communication cultures and encouraging diverse stakeholders to participate can broaden the scope of outreach strategies and have a positive impact on communities (Figure 6.1).

Open data offers significant capacity-building opportunities and can indirectly benefit individuals supported by organizations utilizing it. For instance, in marginalized areas, enhancing the skills of entrepreneurs can address the brain drain phenomenon. By attracting new talents and improving the workforce, employability, and investment, open data contributes to creating a better quality of life in those localities.

WHAT CAN YOU DO....

FIND A DATASET THAT HAS THE POTENTIAL TO MAKE AN IMPACT

DEVELOP NARRATIVES TO EXPLAIN THE DATASET IN A WAY THAT RESONATES WITH SOCIAL ACTION

DEMONSTRATE PRACTICAL WAYS TO USE THE DATA, SUCH AS FOR FUNDING OR CAMPAIGNING EVIDENCE

ESTABLISH METRICS FOR MAPPING IMPACT. IT CAN BE AS SIMPLE AS USING A SPREADSHEET

SHARE YOUR LEARNING, FOR EXAMPLE, BY WRITING A BLOG

FIGURE 6.1   What are the steps you should consider when creating narratives?

In my opinion, "public value" plays a central role in the debate concerning open data, and we can reshape its public image. Incorporating public value thinking into open data outreach strategies is crucial for maximizing its benefits for community projects. Understanding and defining "public value" allows us to create frameworks that empower citizens, promote meaningful engagement, and enhance the overall welfare of society.

NOTES

1   Annenberg School for Communication, University of Pennsylvania. (n.d.). Populism in the Twenty-First Century. Annenberg School for Communication. https://amc.sas.upenn.edu/cas-mudde-populism-twenty-first-century

2   Christensen, C. M., Raynor, M., & McDonald, R. (2015). *What Is Disruptive Innovation?* Harvard Business Review.

3   Crosby, B. C., 't Hart, P., & Torfing, J. (2016). Public value creation through collaborative innovation. *Public Management Review*, 18(5), 655–669. https://doi.org/10.1080/14719037.2016.1192165

Open Data for Fundraising

7

Is It More Important than Ever? Building Capacity and Learning from the COVID-19 Aftermath

The world is a volatile place; one second we are in good stead and everything is falling into place; we have clear objectives; we can start to map what the future could look like; and that 5-year plan we made a few years ago is looking like everything is going to come to fruition. Life is good, right?

And then, like a volcano erupting, life changes; those outcomes and priorities have changed, and that 5-year plan you made has gone completely out of the window.

That is exactly what happened to our charity and voluntary organizations during the COVID-19 crisis, and it's not going to get any easier for them over the next 10–15 years as we emerge from the pandemic.

Why? Many of these charity and community organizations rely on core funding from local governments or health providers, such as the NHS in the UK, for example. With more priorities to address and less money available than before, and considering that budgets were already tight, the situation became even more challenging.

In short, a lot of these organizations are going to need to justify their basis for funding. This isn't a conspiracy theory; unfortunately, this is something very real, and we need to take this seriously because this could happen again, and we need to learn from it.

To reiterate, community resilience is imperative, and for a community to be resilient, especially on a hyper-local level, these organizations are more important than ever, as real people depend on them, and most importantly, they are the experts of that locality as they live there.

The essence of community resilience is for that neighborhood, town, or city to have everything they need to withstand and recover from adverse situations. On a hyperlocal

DOI: 10.1201/9781032724645-7

level, especially in low-income areas, charities and third-sector organizations are the centers of their universe, especially in faith-based communities. It's not an overstatement to say that residents depend on them, and if these projects close their doors, that could be the difference from people getting support to truly feeling isolated.

UK cross-party think tank, Demos, in their 2021 report, said[1]:

> Without urgent and targeted intervention, grassroots charity organizations—those less likely to have adequate reserves—risk being wiped out altogether. At the same time, public giving throughout the crisis risks being used as a stopgap to fill widening deficiencies in statutory provision.

Smaller third-sector grassroots organizations need to improve their capacity and, in some ways, need to be better than their larger counterparts—there is an old saying that to be a good social entrepreneur, you need to be better than the private sector equivalent, as it is harder to set up, it's tougher to make a living, and your selling model is much smaller. You can't send a marketing flyer to a government, can you? Post-2020s, this is truer than ever.

In 2020, the then UK Chancellor of the Exchequer, Rishi Sunak, announced the £750m^2 Coronavirus Community Support Fund, which was targeted at "small and medium-sized charities" working "at the heart of local communities."

But an Independent Government report in partnership with UK grant giver, The National Lottery, stated: "Around 23% of the total funding was given to charities with an income between £10,000 and £100,000, and 47% went to charities with an income between £100,000 and £1m^3."

It's worth noting that a lot of funding applications that grant givers receive from the third sector aren't bad ideas; proposals are just poorly put together and do not evidence the need, and funders regularly talk about struggling to find quality applications—in my eyes, that is a capacity issue; this could be the skills that are just not there, which larger NGOs may have in abundance.

The least we can do is give them all the tools they need to fight their way out of a bad situation. If we lived in a perfect world, charities would not need to offer rationales so they could receive core funding, but we don't, and if there are mechanisms that can help them, surely it's easy enough to share information with them (Figure 7.1).

This is why community-based capacity-building training, such as using open data, is now more important than ever before, and in an uncertain world, smaller and grassroots NGOs and charities need to understand the reality of what they face going forward.

Crucially, they are vital to residents in neighborhoods that have a range of issues, sometimes highly technical issues, especially areas with a high diaspora of ethnic minorities. For instance, in the West Midlands, there is a small town called Smethwick, which has a population of just over 50,000 and has over 100 languages spoken over such a small area. That is a lot of tailored support, and there are places like this all over the world.

Furthermore, from a mental health point of view, we have to consider that during the COVID-19 pandemic, a lot of people were locked up in their homes, which led to unprecedented levels of people coming forward with cases of anxiety and depression.

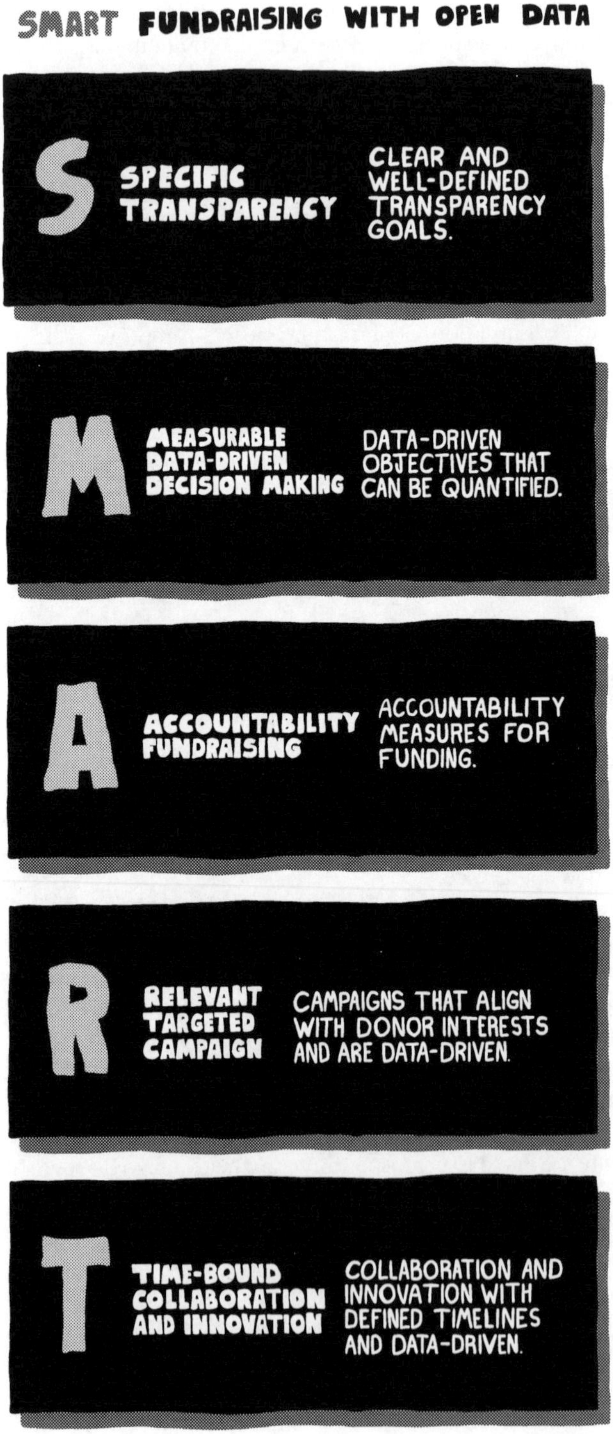

SMART FUNDRAISING WITH OPEN DATA

S — SPECIFIC TRANSPARENCY — CLEAR AND WELL-DEFINED TRANSPARENCY GOALS.

M — MEASURABLE DATA-DRIVEN DECISION MAKING — DATA-DRIVEN OBJECTIVES THAT CAN BE QUANTIFIED.

A — ACCOUNTABILITY FUNDRAISING — ACCOUNTABILITY MEASURES FOR FUNDING.

R — RELEVANT TARGETED CAMPAIGN — CAMPAIGNS THAT ALIGN WITH DONOR INTERESTS AND ARE DATA-DRIVEN.

T — TIME-BOUND COLLABORATION AND INNOVATION — COLLABORATION AND INNOVATION WITH DEFINED TIMELINES AND DATA-DRIVEN.

FIGURE 7.1   Steps to consider using the SMART method.

You have to ask yourself: What does support mean on the ground to residents? Is it policies made by our elected officials or something tangible that can be seen and touched? I'd suggest it is the latter, and in the face of real issues caused by health-related social exclusion and poverty—the institutions that are best placed to attempt to fix our society moving forward and attenuate community issues are these community organizations.

Using open data as a basis for funding is a process I feel all community organizations should learn. Using it as a basis of evidence for what the social need is, the evidence of how it affects your community, and how you will use that data to track your impact is an excellent foundation for a tendering application, because if that data is open, they can check for themselves.

You need to set out a good argument in a funding application to ensure that you have a good chance of being awarded the money. I always approach funding tenders looking for ways to argue with what I want to change and then how I can refute that argument, but if you think about it, how can they argue with facts? Those are just a few of the questions I ask myself before I press submit. Our funding tenders must be watertight concerning evidence.

It's not like they would come back to you and expect you to defend yourself, but they may ask if you could expand on certain areas, and if you can simply present them with the cold, hard facts and explain how your project would help to alleviate that, that will take away the needless stress of you having to think of content to debate your point; you'd just need to talk them through the application.

Renowned social tech writer and Editor at Large for Wired, Steven Levy, once famously said, "You can't argue with facts. You're not entitled to your facts.[4]"

Okay, let's backtrack for a minute, as it might make more sense if I gave some narrative here.

Let's think of some scenarios that could give you an idea of how non-tech-savvy NGOs could use open data as a basis for fundraising. Let me elaborate, as perhaps it can still seem a bit complex, and being able to present you with ways you can use to explain open data to the third sector is something I want you to understand.

In the UK, it's quite common for residents in marginalized areas to get together to form a legal not-for-profit entity that can represent the views and interests of the people who live in their housing estate or area; these are called Tenants and Residents Associations (TRAs). If a TRA in a social housing estate in Cornwall, England, for example, is looking to win some money from a local grant-giving organization to fund a project that looks to raise awareness about the rise of anti-social behavior in their neighborhood over the last 6 months, they could evidence this problem by searching their ward on the UK Police website that presents live monthly crime data and use that as the foundation to give credence to their funding application.

Climate change is a prevalent issue for every corner of the globe, but for small island nations such as the Maldives, it's a case of life and death for their country, as in, they will not exist if something very drastic is done soon. A youth charity in the country is applying for government money to create a lesson plan that can be taught in neighboring Asian nation schools to showcase what climate change means to them and why it is important to think about these issues as they get older. They are using open data from the Climate Control Coastal Risk Screening Tool as a basis to form the lesson, which showcases that by 2030, large parts of the country will disappear and then vanish by 2090.

In Uganda, a wildlife conservation charity is seeking international funding to protect endangered species such as mountain gorillas. They use open data from the International Union for Conservation of Nature (IUCN) to demonstrate the declining population of these gorillas, emphasizing the urgency of their conservation efforts.

The South American nation of Chile has a real issue with child obesity, topping lists across the continent, so a charity focused on health aims to tackle the alarming rates of childhood obesity and related health concerns. By utilizing open data from the World Health Organization (WHO), they craft informative infographics and reports that shed light on concerning trends and health risks, seeking support from both government and private donors.

In response to previous major natural disasters, a disaster relief charity in Japan is seeking funding to bolster its preparedness efforts. By harnessing open data from the Japan Meteorological Agency, they bring attention to the escalating frequency of such calamities, emphasizing the critical significance of disaster risk reduction initiatives.

Tangible and relatable examples are a great way to explain how open data can work in practice for funding. When I run training, I regularly add examples such as this to my presentations.

This is the part when I want to come back to push the idea of using open data for funding, and I really would like every third sector and voluntary organization to do this and add value to their work. It's not as complicated as you would believe; if you have a clear outlook of the type of data you need to firm up the need to solve the social issue, you will find it, and if you can't, go to your local authority and request it.

Open data also serves as a powerful tool for third-sector organizations to measure their impact; it meticulously assesses and articulates the transformative changes they bring to communities. By harnessing data, organizations can track and quantify the outcomes of their initiatives, demonstrating to potential donors the tangible difference they make in people's lives. Whether it's showcasing the number of lives improved, communities strengthened, or social issues addressed, the transparency and credibility offered by open data enable organizations to tell compelling impact stories that resonate with those willing to support their cause.

You do not have to be an expert on open data to use it; you just need to figure out what you need it for and go from there—it's a bit like going on vacation and you want to learn a little bit of the native language to get by. You do not need to be fluent to ask for the bill, do you?

In short, do not get bogged down with the confusing hyperbole around open data, focus on what you need it for and stay on that path.

USING AI CHATBOTS TO HELP WRITE FUNDING APPLICATIONS

There is one powerful and highly simple tool out there that can help you write funding tenders based on analyzed data—something so easy you can copy and paste in raw data along with prompts of what you want it to do.

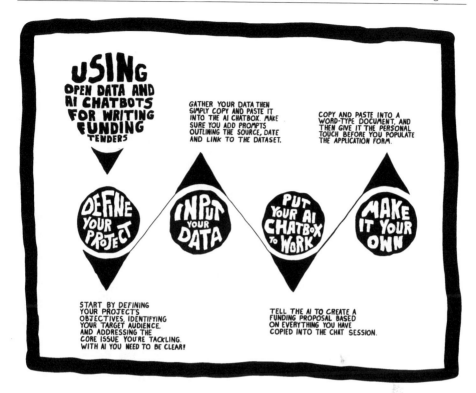

FIGURE 7.2   An illustration outlining how we can mix open data and AI chatbots to create funding applications.

AI chatbots are what you make of them. You can ask them to do all sorts of stupid stuff, but for busy grassroots workers or social activists, they can act as a capacity-building lifeline.

As the old saying goes, "work smarter, not harder," is very apt for this section. Civil society organizations being more "smart" is a broader argument—this is the case for the third sector to utilize all of the digital tools at their disposal. And as random as it may seem, AI chatbots could just be one of those tools. Some might say it's cheating, but if it frees up your capacity for people to concentrate on the value that their work offers to citizens, I, for one, am okay with that (Figure 7.2).

Let's touch on this so it is clear.

IDENTIFYING TRENDS WITH OPEN DATASETS

Suppose you need to identify trends in your area, like changes in educational needs. You can easily input your query and copy relevant data from various sources, such as government websites or educational statistics, to the AI chatbot. The chatbot will then process your request and provide you with insights if it identifies any noteworthy trends, like a growing demand for educational support. This equips nonprofits to devise customized solutions for local challenges, all founded on thorough data analysis.

WRITING FUNDING APPLICATIONS

AI chatbots can help with a lot of the legwork in crafting grant applications. Let's say your nonprofit is on a mission to secure funding for a new initiative aimed at enhancing digital skills among older individuals in your community. First, provide essential details about the program, such as what you plan to do and its objectives, the specific digital skill needs within your community, and any relevant supporting data. The chatbot takes this information and composes a basic grant proposal, making a persuasive case for why your project merits funding. You act as the guide, sharing the specifics, while the chatbot does the heavy lifting, and then you change it accordingly.

GENERATING REPORTS BASED ON LOCAL OPEN DATA

They can also be helpful regarding report generation, simplifying your workload. Imagine you lead a local environmental group and want to share an annual report highlighting improvements in air quality in your city. You can input data from air quality monitors into the chatbot, along with explanations and key findings. The chatbot then assembles all this information into a report.

AI chatbots aren't the answer to everything. It means you will need to be more creative with your ideas, but you can be sure your counterparts will be doing this. Why not you, at least to help you in the beginning? But please take away that you need to make these processes your own. These are just conduits to make the first step easier.

Finishing up, harnessing open data is vital for charities and voluntary organizations seeking funding and evidence-based support. Begin by identifying relevant data sources, understanding their nuances, and effectively visualizing the information. Craft a compelling narrative that aligns the data with your project's goals and engages with local authorities when necessary. Building data capacity within your organization and consistently demonstrating the impact of your initiatives will enhance your ability to secure funding and make a real difference in your community. Open data is a powerful tool that can drive positive change when used strategically.

NOTES

1 Demos. (2021, January). The Impact of the COVID-19 Pandemic on the Charitable Sector, and Its Prospects for Recovery. https://demos.co.uk/wp-content/uploads/2021/01/Covid-19-impact-on-the-charitable-sector.pdf

2 UK Government. (2021, April 8). Chancellor Sets Out Extra £750 Million Coronavirus Funding for Frontline Charities. GOV.UK. https://www.gov.uk/government/news/chancellor-sets-out-extra-750-million-coronavirus-funding-for-frontline-charities#:~:text=News%20story-,Chancellor%20sets%20out%20extra%20%C2%A3750%20million%20coronavirus%20funding%20for,today%20(Wednesday%208%20April)

3 Mackay, S., Bierman, R., Craston, M., & Mastrogregori, E. (2021, July). Process Evaluation of the Coronavirus Community Support Fund (CCSF) Final Report. The National Lottery Community Fund. https://www.tnlcommunityfund.org.uk/media/insights/documents/CCSF_FINAL_Process_Report _ 050721 _ PUBLISHED.pdf?mtime=20210705135158&focal=none

4 Levy, S. (2011). *In the Plex: How Google Thinks, Works, and Shapes Our Lives.* ISBN: 9781416596585.

Data without Security Is Like a Ship without a Captain—Adrift and Vulnerable

8

Open data can be the key to collaborative innovation, but remember, doors that have precious things behind them need good locks—data security is your padlock.

It's not an uncommon sight when we watch the news to hear stories of massive businesses suffering from data breaches, hackers breaking their barriers and using that data for no good, either selling it to marketing corporations on the black market and scammers or using it as leverage against the organization in question.

With open data, it's slightly different because, in essence, you are happy to share that data, but that doesn't mean you have to disregard keeping your data safe (Figure 8.1).

Every dataset carries a vision, a hope that it will serve a specific purpose, ideally contributing to the betterment of your community. However, security isn't just about procedures to safeguard data; it's also about crystal-clear guidelines on how you intend the data to be used, accompanied by a comprehensive outline of your dataset's terms and conditions.

Privacy protection stands as an utmost concern for open data. Under the expansive landscape of open data, personal and sensitive information often lies in wait, vulnerable to exploitation. Failing to diligently protect this data can yield severe consequences, ranging from privacy violations to the far-reaching implications of identity theft and other potential harms to individuals. Consequently, robust data security measures have become imperative and essential for maintaining the integrity and trustworthiness of open data initiatives.

At the core of open data lies integrity, an unwavering cornerstone demanding relentless attention. The accuracy and reliability of open data are non-negotiable, for any tampering or manipulation can send waves of misinformation cascading through decision-making processes and public understanding. Inaccurate data can lead to misguided conclusions, which, in turn, may trigger potentially harmful actions. Preserving

DOI: 10.1201/9781032724645-8

FIGURE 8.1   A snapshot of data security basics.

data integrity isn't merely a best practice; it's imperative to ensure that open data effectively and responsibly serves its intended purpose.

Trust and credibility form the lifeblood of open data initiatives, hinging on the belief that data is not just accessible but also secure. Compromised data security shakes the very foundation of trust in the organizations or governments driving these initiatives. Such breaches erode confidence not only in the data but also discourage individuals and entities from engaging in open data projects. The perception of insecurity becomes a formidable barrier, hindering the full potential of open data in fostering transparency, innovation, and collaboration, making it absolutely essential to uphold the trustworthiness of these initiatives.

As we emphasized in our chapter on opening up your data, it is crucial to underscore that legal compliance serves as a cornerstone of responsible open data management.

Organizations entrusted with open data must shoulder the responsibility of strict adherence to data protection laws and regulations. These are not mere recommendations but legal mandates, carrying significant consequences for non-compliance, including substantial fines and potential legal proceedings. To fortify the integrity of open data initiatives and proactively address these risks, organizations must possess an in-depth understanding of the legal landscape and exhibit an unwavering commitment to data protection prerequisites.

You need to ensure your data has no personal indicators; otherwise, you could be in for a world of trouble. This misuse encompasses identity theft, fraud, cyberattacks, and targeted exploitation, and that is something you really don't want to come back to haunt your organization. Open data, when combined with other sources, becomes a potent tool for crafting sophisticated attacks and deceiving individuals and organizations. Vigilance, robust data anonymization, stringent access controls, vigilant monitoring, education, and meticulous incident response planning stand as formidable defenses against the potential malevolence lurking in open data, preserving its integrity and safeguarding those it serves.

And when the security of open data falters, its consequences often extend far beyond the digital world. Such incidents leave an indelible mark on the reputation of the organization responsible for the data release. They trigger public backlash, erode trust, and inflict profound damage to credibility. This tarnish not only sullies an organization's standing but also hinders its capacity to champion transparency, innovation, and collaboration through open data initiatives. Safeguarding data integrity, therefore, transcends mere responsibility; it serves as a bulwark against the profound reputational costs that may follow data misuse.

But what can you do?

In the face of potential data misuse within open data environments, proactive measures are imperative. Thoroughly anonymize personally identifiable information before releasing data, ensuring individuals remain unidentifiable. Implement robust access controls, limiting open data access to authorized personnel. Vigilantly monitor data usage patterns to promptly identify suspicious activities. Educate users on responsible data use, emphasizing privacy and compliance with data protection laws. Lastly, develop an incident response plan outlining the steps to take in case of data misuse, including reporting to relevant authorities and affected individuals.

So all this is well and good, and I'm fully aware some technical language has been used here, and I completely appreciate that you are probably by no means a data scientist, you are here to learn about what it can look like without the hyperbole, so let's create a case study of what this can look like in real terms.

SCENARIO: DATA BREACH INCIDENT AND PUBLIC FALLOUT IN PARAMARIBO, SURINAME

In this fictional scenario, an advocacy group in Paramaribo, Suriname, initiated a project to collect and share data on local skills gaps within communities, intending to release the data as open data through their website. However, due to lapses in data security measures and the inadvertent inclusion of personal indicators such as names and income levels, a data breach occurred. Subsequently, the breach became the subject of a critical story published by a local newspaper, damaging the organization's reputation and trust within the community.

PROBLEM DESCRIPTION

The NGO encountered several issues that contributed to the data breach on their open data website:

Inadequate Data Security Measures: The NGO did not implement robust data security measures on their website, leaving the data vulnerable to unauthorized access.

Inadequate Data Anonymization: The organization failed to properly anonymize the data, leading to the inclusion of personal indicators like names and income levels in the open dataset.

HOW THE BREACH OCCURRED

The breach occurred because the NGO neglected to secure its open data website adequately. As a result, an unauthorized individual gained access to the dataset and extracted sensitive information, including personal identifiers.

CONSEQUENCES

The consequences of this data breach were multifaceted:

Privacy Violations: The breach led to the exposure of personal information, including individuals' names and income levels, which should have been anonymized to protect their privacy.

Data Accuracy: The breach raised concerns about the accuracy of the data, as unauthorized changes or manipulation might have occurred.

Trust Erosion: Users and stakeholders lost trust in the organization's open data initiatives due to the breach, impacting their willingness to contribute to or engage with future projects.

Reputational Damage: The incident damaged the NGO's reputation as a reliable data custodian and advocate for community welfare, affecting its credibility.

PUBLIC FALLOUT

Following the data breach, a local newspaper in Paramaribo published a critical story that exposed the breach of trust and highlighted the shortcomings in the NGO's data management practices. The story garnered public attention and scrutiny, further intensifying the reputational damage to the organization. The community's faith in the NGO's commitment to safeguarding their data and welfare was severely shaken.

PREVENTIVE MEASURES

To thwart such breaches and safeguard sensitive information hosted on their website, the advocacy group could have implemented a series of preventive measures:

Data Anonymization: Employ meticulous data anonymization techniques for any data containing personal information on their website, preventing the identification of individuals by removing or replacing sensitive details.

Training and Awareness: Offer comprehensive training to staff on data security best practices, emphasizing strong password usage, the recognition of phishing attempts, and secure data handling protocols, especially in the context of their website.

Regular Security Audits for Their Website: Conduct periodic security audits and assessments of their website to identify vulnerabilities and weaknesses in the data handling process. Promptly address any identified issues.

Incident Response Plan: Develop a clearly defined incident response plan outlining the steps to be taken in the event of a data breach on their website. This includes notifying affected individuals and relevant authorities in compliance with data protection regulations.

Data Retention Policy for Their Website: Implement a data retention policy for data hosted on their website, specifying the duration for which data should be retained and the secure deletion or archiving procedures.

By proactively implementing these security measures for their website, the NGO could have significantly reduced the risk of data breaches, safeguarding both the privacy and security of those involved in their surveys. This not only ensures compliance with data protection regulations but also upholds the integrity of their open data initiative, specifically on their website.

Now that you have an overview of privacy, let's delve deeper into data compliance and regulation. These two areas are interconnected, and in the next chapter, we will explore some of the legal complexities and behaviors while providing you with an overview of the current landscape.

Data Self-Defense

Data Compliance and Regulation

9

Are you the kind of person who hops onto a website, let's say, to indulge in some serious dog memes? You're practically smashing your thumb against the screen just to banish those pesky cookie alerts, all for the sake of that sweet meme bounty. But at the same time—when it's your banking app sending out a terms and conditions update, you're suddenly reading it as meticulously as if it were your last will and testament.

You might be the type of person who casually shares certain data about themselves on social media but also voices concerns when discussing data sharing with friends. And when you hear about data breaches, it triggers those prangs of digital anxiety.

Well, did you know this is a thing? It is called the "Privacy Paradox."[1]

It is a rather intriguing phenomenon in the context of online behavior. It revolves around the perplexing inconsistency between what people express and what they actually do concerning their privacy when navigating the vast expanse of the internet. You see, many users vocally voice their concerns about the privacy of their personal information while using online platforms. They'll emphatically declare their worries, but their actions often tell a completely different story. For instance, social media—they willingly divulge sensitive details here and on other websites, even though they've been vocal about their concerns regarding data privacy.

This curious behavior tends to be particularly noticeable in arenas such as online shopping, social networks, and mobile apps. In an attempt to fathom this paradox, researchers have offered up various theories. Some suggest it's all about users consciously weighing the pros and cons of sharing their information—a rational approach. Others believe that cognitive biases come into play, influencing how people make decisions in the online sphere. Despite all these theories, there's still no one-size-fits-all explanation for the privacy paradox. It remains an ongoing enigma in the world of online privacy behavior, keeping researchers engaged in lively debates and tireless quests for answers (Figure 9.1).

DOI: 10.1201/9781032724645-9

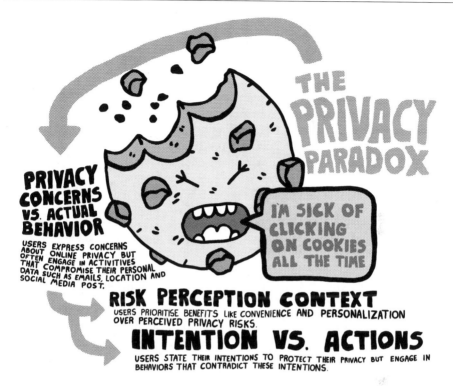

FIGURE 9.1   How does the privacy paradox manifests itself.

I am not going to lie; from working with community organizations, I often see glazed-over looks staring back at me when I start talking about data protection. I am fully aware that this topic can be about as interesting as watching paint dry.

But it doesn't have to be; data protection can be easier and more straightforward than you think. Also, it's important; in fact, it's absolutely crucial. So if your thumb is twitching to skip this chapter, calm that digit because we are about to go on a wild ride that is all about protecting your data. Still with me? Let's go.

You might not be jumping with excitement, but understanding this topic is essential, and no discussion of open data is complete without it. In this chapter, I will lay out what you need to know, what the language means, and what you can do to protect yourself and your organization.

To gain a deeper insight into data protection, let's embark on a journey centered on the European Union (EU), renowned for its comprehensive approach, which has influenced many nations worldwide. While we'll touch on global counterparts, these regulations share common threads.

At the heart of data protection lies the EU's formidable regulation: the General Data Protection Regulation,[2] or GDPR for short. It was born out of concerns regarding the privacy of EU citizens and the transfer of personal data, ultimately setting stringent data protection standards (Figure 9.2).

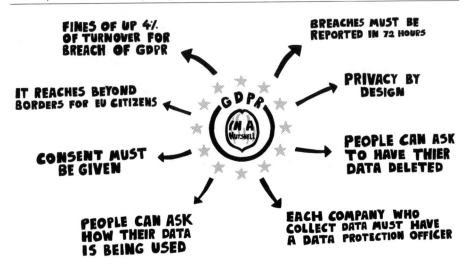

FINES OF UP 4%.
OF TURNOVER FOR
BREACH OF GDPR

BREACHES MUST BE
REPORTED IN 72 HOURS

PRIVACY BY
DESIGN

IT REACHES BEYOND
BORDERS FOR EU CITIZENS

GDPR
(IN A Nutshell)

PEOPLE CAN ASK
TO HAVE THIER
DATA DELETED

CONSENT MUST
BE GIVEN

PEOPLE CAN ASK
HOW THEIR DATA
IS BEING USED

EACH COMPANY WHO
COLLECT DATA MUST HAVE
A DATA PROTECTION OFFICER

FIGURE 9.2   What is GDPR, in a nutshell?

GDPR emerged as a direct response to the aftermath of the Safe Harbor framework's demise.[3] Safe Harbor, in simpler terms, was an agreement that smoothed the way for companies to transfer personal data from the European Union to the United States. It meant they didn't have to go through additional bureaucratic hurdles with EU authorities. However, there was a caveat—US companies had to commit to safeguarding individuals' data by adhering to certain principles. These principles included providing transparent information to individuals about data processing, offering choices, ensuring data security, maintaining data accuracy, allowing data access, and establishing mechanisms for enforcement.

Then came the year 2015, when the European Court of Justice (ECJ) declared the Safe Harbor agreement invalid.[4] Why? Well, the main gripe was that it failed to provide adequate protection for the personal data of EU citizens against potential surveillance by US government agencies. You see, US legislation at the time allowed these agencies access to personal data held by US companies, even if the data originated from the EU.

The ECJ's ruling sent shockwaves through companies accustomed to transferring data from the EU to the US. They were left with no choice but to swiftly adapt their data transfer practices to ensure compliance with EU regulations.

It kind of proved the EU right if you fast forward to the Cambridge Analytica scandal[5] with the unauthorized collection of Facebook users' data for political profiling and targeting, which shook the foundations of data privacy and its utilization in political contexts. This incident triggered intensified scrutiny of data transfer practices between the EU and the US. It underscored the critical importance of protecting personal data, especially when it intersects with political affairs. This ongoing evolution of data protection standards remains at the forefront of global privacy discussions.

GDPR serves as the blueprint, establishing the legal framework for organizations to handle personal data responsibly. Entities subject to GDPR must craft their own data protection policies, outlining how they collect, store, process, and safeguard personal data in alignment with GDPR standards.

Key elements of GDPR grant individuals (known as data subjects) various rights, including access to their data, the right to rectify it, the renowned "right to be forgotten," and data portability. For organizations handling substantial personal or sensitive data, GDPR may necessitate the appointment of a Data Protection Officer to ensure compliance.

A fundamental principle revolves around obtaining clear, informed, and freely given consent from individuals before processing their data, forming the foundation of GDPR's approach. In cases of data breaches, organizations must promptly notify relevant authorities and affected individuals, prioritizing transparency and accountability.

You may need a safety net to help you here, and that's where a Data Protection Impact Assessment (DPIA) comes in. They are like safety check-ups for important data tasks that carry some risks. They help organizations spot any possible problems and figure out how to make them less risky. Being responsible is a big deal, and GDPR says we need to write down how we handle data, create rules to protect it, and regularly double-check everything to ensure it's safe.

GDPR's reach extends beyond the EU, encompassing the transfer of personal data outside its borders and imposing specific safeguards and conditions. Non-compliance can result in substantial fines, with penalties reaching up to 4% of a company's global annual revenue or €20 million, whichever is higher.

Meta, the owner of Facebook, has been fined multiple times for breaching GDPR rules. The Irish Data Protection Commission (DPC) made a historic decision in May 2023. They imposed a monumental fine of €1.2 billion.[6] The fine was imposed for inadequately protecting the personal data of European users during transfers to the United States, marking a major milestone in data protection regulation.

To simplify operations for multinational organizations, GDPR introduces a "one-stop-shop" mechanism, enabling them to primarily engage with one Data Protection Authority (DPA) for cross-border data protection matters.

The impact of GDPR resonates globally, influencing data protection practices worldwide. Various countries, including the USA, Canada, Brazil, and China, have developed their own distinct regulations, showcasing differences in jurisdiction, data subject rights, data transfer mechanisms, and penalties. Navigating this diverse landscape is vital for organizations embracing data protection in our interconnected world.

Some countries insist on data remaining within their borders, a concept absent from GDPR. This divergence poses unique challenges for global NGOs striving to comply with varying data storage requirements.

Penalties for data protection breaches differ across regions. GDPR wields significant fines, while other nations may impose distinct scales and enforcement approaches, underscoring the importance of understanding regulations within each jurisdiction.

Data Protection Authorities (DPAs), the custodians of data protection, vary from one country to another, each with varying levels of authority and resources. These institutions play a pivotal role in ensuring compliance and safeguarding individual privacy (Figure 9.3).

FIGURE 9.3   What should you consider when you run a data protection impact assessment?

Cultural and legal influences further enrich the global data protection landscape. Different nations blend their unique cultural norms and legal traditions into their data protection laws.

China's approach to data privacy is quite fascinating due to its two distinctive components, notably the concept of "cyber-sovereignty" (which we'll delve into further in the upcoming chapter) and the differentiation between private privacy and state privacy.[7]

First, "private security," is an individual's ability to maintain the confidentiality of their personal information and activities. It ensures that their personal data, which encompasses details such as contact information, financial records, and online browsing habits, remains safeguarded against unauthorized access or utilization, be it by corporations or individuals.

Then we have "state privacy," centered on shielding an individual's personal information and activities from government authorities or agencies. It establishes that governments cannot infringe upon citizens' private lives without valid justifications, such as national security concerns or law enforcement necessities.

The United States has less strict data privacy compared to the European Union and China models anyway. They take a sectoral approach,[8] and there is not an all-encompassing federally legislated measure, meaning healthcare, finance, education, and telecommunications all have their own data privacy regulations—this is not seen as comprehensive as its counterparts because protection differs from the sector and it clearly can be convoluted.

This model relies on self-regulation in large part, meaning they expect companies to voluntarily agree to certain privacy and regulations. And then the Federal Trade Commission, which is responsible for protecting consumers and promoting competition in the marketplace, monitors them.

From an American point of view, it is not great reading; however, it is not all bad; it is worth checking out your state's data privacy laws. For example, the California Consumer Privacy Act (CCPA)[9] and the Virginia Consumer Data Protection Act (VCDPA)[10] offer stronger protections, both laws enforcing businesses to be transparent in regards to data collection and what they plan to do with it. They are enforced by state attorney generals who have the power to investigate and bring lawsuits against corporations that they feel have broken the laws, giving consumers more power over their digital rights.

In certain regions, data protection resembles a patchwork quilt, with some countries introducing sector-specific data protection laws in addition to overarching privacy laws. In contrast, GDPR casts a wider net, covering a broader spectrum of data processing activities.

Inspiration knows no borders, as evident in GDPR-inspired laws emerging in countries such as Brazil and South Korea. These regulations, infused with GDPR's principles and concepts, signify the growing global influence of Europe's data protection guidelines.

What all these agree on, regardless of whether it is executed or voluntary, is data compliance. It is not just seen as a necessity; it is an important step to protecting our digital rights.

So, if you're planning to release data in any manner, a data compliance policy is a must. Fear not, as I'm here to assist, with a focus tailored to the world of open data.

DATA COMPLIANCE POLICY

INTRODUCTION

At [Your Organization's Name], we are deeply committed to safeguarding the privacy of individuals whose data we process. We adhere to the principles outlined in the General Data Protection Regulation (GDPR) to ensure the responsible handling of personal information. This policy outlines our approach to data protection and compliance with GDPR.

DATA RECORDS

We keep records detailing why we collect data and with whom it is shared. This helps us maintain transparency and accountability in our data processing activities.

Develop a simple system for documenting data processing activities within your organization.

DATA RETENTION

We decide how long we retain data, ensuring it aligns with GDPR guidelines and the specific purposes for which data was collected.

Establish clear data retention periods that suit your organization's needs and align with GDPR recommendations.

PRIVACY NOTICES

We provide clear and concise privacy notices when collecting data to ensure individuals understand how their information will be used.

Create template privacy notices that are easily customizable for various data collection scenarios.

LAWFUL DATA PROCESSING

We process data based on lawful reasons, including consent, contract, legal obligation, and more.

Document the specific legal basis for data processing in different contexts within your organization.

ACCESS REQUESTS

We assist individuals in accessing their data when requested, verifying their identity as needed.

Develop a streamlined process for handling access requests while ensuring data subject verification.

PRIVACY CONSIDERATION

We prioritize privacy when designing systems or processes, and we only collect data that is necessary for our organizational purposes.

Consider conducting privacy impact assessments (PIAs) for new projects or initiatives.

MINIMAL DATA

We emphasize the collection of only necessary data and actively work to minimize data collection.

Conduct a data audit to identify and eliminate unnecessary data collection.

THIRD-PARTY PARTNERS

We collaborate with partners who also adhere to GDPR principles to ensure data security and compliance.

Vet third-party partners to confirm GDPR compliance.

DATA SECURITY

We implement security measures based on the importance of the data we handle.

Implement security measures appropriate for the types of data you handle. Data Breach:

BREACH REPORTING

We have a process in place for reporting data breaches and ensuring transparency and compliance with GDPR requirements.

Develop an incident response plan outlining steps to take in case of a data breach.

POLICY UPDATES

We commit to regularly reviewing and updating this policy to stay compliant with evolving regulations.

Set a schedule for policy reviews and updates that align with your organizational needs.

CONCLUSION

At [Your Organization's Name], data privacy and GDPR compliance are at the core of our operations. We are dedicated to protecting personal information and ensuring transparency in all our data processing activities.

Signature: [Authorised Signatory]

Date: [Insert Date]

Data privacy is a paramount concern for organizations of all sizes, including small third-sector nonprofits. Whether you're planning a new project or assessing an ongoing activity, safeguarding personal information is not only good practice but also a legal requirement under regulations such as the General Data Protection Regulation.

To help you protect data effectively you should consider conducting a data privacy assessment on the data you already have or to set the precedent of what you plan to collect.

Every data privacy assessment begins with a clear understanding of your project or activity, so let us look at this from the angle of setting up a project and you are putting protection methods in place.

Start by providing a brief description of what it entails and why it's essential. This initial step ensures that your endeavor aligns with your organization's objectives.

Now, consider why this project or activity is necessary. Does it contribute to your overarching goals? Ensuring alignment with your organization's mission is crucial to justify the need for data processing.

List the types of information you'll be handling during this project. Understand where this data comes from and where it's destined to go. This knowledge helps you better protect and manage this information.

Privacy is a collective responsibility. Identify individuals or groups who might be affected by or knowledgeable about your project. Seek their input to improve your approach and address privacy concerns effectively.

Identify potential privacy issues that might arise during your project. Evaluate how severe these issues could be. Develop a plan to mitigate or prevent these problems, and consider necessary changes to enhance data privacy practices.

Document every step of your assessment and action plan. Share this documentation with relevant stakeholders for approval. Ensure unanimous agreement on the proposed data privacy measures.

Put your plan into action. Execute the steps you've outlined to protect data privacy. Continuously monitor the progress of your project and assess whether your data protection measures remain effective.

Keep detailed records of your data privacy efforts. If any issues or deviations occur, make sure to report them. Transparency is key in maintaining data privacy standards.

By following these simplified steps, your organization can uphold data privacy while pursuing your mission. Remember that data protection is an ongoing commitment that requires diligence and dedication.

Regulating your data is the new normal if you run any kind of entity, and the third sector needs to excel in it more than anybody else. So, when you have your business hat on, there is no place for the privacy paradox to seep into your work, regardless of how boring it may seem.

The landscape of data laws will change rapidly over the years, but it is clear that the Europeans distrust corporations, the Americans do not trust their government[11] and the Chinese[12] don't trust either corporations or the government. From a central level, it can get pretty murky, but good practice starts at home, meaning there is nothing stopping us from showing the big guys how it is done.

NOTES

1 Barth, S., & De Jong, M. D. (2017). The privacy paradox–Investigating discrepancies between expressed privacy concerns and actual online behavior–A systematic literature review. *Telematics and Informatics*, 34(7), 1038–1058.
2 European Parliament, & Council of the European Union. (2016). Regulation (EU) 2016/679 of the European Parliament and of the Council of 27 April 2016 on the protection of natural persons with regard to the processing of personal data and on the free movement of such data, and repealing Directive 95/46/EC (General Data Protection Regulation). EUR-Lex. https://eur-lex.europa.eu/eli/reg/2016/679
3 Ni Loideain, N. (2016). The end of safe harbor: Implications for EU digital privacy and data protection law. *Journal of Internet Law*, 19(8).

4 Padova, Y. (2016). The Safe Harbour is invalid: What tools remain for data transfers and what comes next? *International Data Privacy Law*, 6(2), 139–161.

5 ur Rehman, I. (2019). Facebook-Cambridge Analytica data harvesting: What you need to know. *Library Philosophy and Practice*, 1–11.

6 Data Privacy Manager. (2023, September 19). 20 Biggest GDPR Fines So Far [2023]. https://dataprivacymanager.net/5-biggest-gdpr-fines-so-far-2020/

7 Pernot-Leplay, E. (2020, May). China's approach on data privacy law: A third way between the U.S. and the E.U.? *The Penn State Journal of Law & International Affairs (JLIA)*. https://elibrary.law.psu.edu/cgi/viewcontent.cgi?params=/context/jlia/article/1244/&path_info=Pernot_Leplay_8.1_49_117.pdf

8 Boyne, S. M. (2018). Data protection in the United States. *The American Journal of Comparative Law*, 66(suppl_1), 299–343.

9 California Attorney General's Office. (2023, May 10). California Consumer Privacy Act (CCPA). https://oag.ca.gov/privacy/ccpa

10 Virginia Office of the Attorney General. (2023, February 2). The Virginia Consumer Data Protection Act ("VCDPA"). https://www.oag.state.va.us/consumer-protection/files/tips-and-info/Virginia-Consumer-Data-Protection-Act-Summary-2-2-23.pdf

11 Boyne, S. (2018). Data Protection in the United States. *The American Journal of Comparative Law*, 66(suppl_1), 299–343.

12 Hao, K. (2020, August 19). Inside China's Unexpected Quest to Protect Data Privacy. *MIT Technology Review*. https://www.technologyreview.com/2020/08/19/1006441/china-data-privacy-hong-yanqing-gdpr/

Data Sovereignty
Where Data Calls Home and It's Digital Borders

10

Open data might seem like a citizen of the earth, a borderless repository that holds a treasure trove of information from around the world. For example, a research scientist in Jamaica can collaborate with a counterpart in Fiji to map genetic markers, or perhaps an architect in the Maldives and Tonga can study local environmental data in the face of urban planning in the time of rising sea levels. The examples I can give you could be pretty endless.

However, data doesn't possess global citizenship; instead, it adheres to the laws and regulations of its country of origin.

In several nations, stringent regulations oversee cross-border data transfers. To use a Chinese open data set in the UK, for example, you must ensure that such data transfers comply with UK data protection laws because China may have different ideas of what should be regulated or not, meaning that data potentially would not be fit for legal use in the UK.

In our constantly evolving digital world, where data circulates as a global currency, the notion of data sovereignty has become a pivotal subject, merging technology, politics, and culture. Similar to historical struggles for control over physical territories, nations are now engaged in a comparable struggle for dominance in their digital realms. This chapter navigates the intricate landscape of data sovereignty, blending historical insights and cultural allusions to illuminate this contemporary challenge.

To understand data sovereignty, we must first grasp its roots. Imagine, for a moment, the ancient city of Alexandria, a beacon of knowledge in the ancient world. The famous Library of Alexandria housed countless scrolls of wisdom from all corners of the Earth. In some ways, this grand repository of knowledge mirrors today's digital world, with data servers replacing scrolls and global networks acting as the library's halls.

In the 3rd century BCE, Pharaoh Ptolemy II Philadelphus founded the Library of Alexandria not only as a repository of knowledge but also as a means of asserting sovereignty over information.[1] By amassing a vast collection of texts from around the world, the library became a symbol of intellectual and cultural power, a testament to the pharaoh's dominion over the wisdom of the ages.

DOI: 10.1201/9781032724645-10

Fast forward to now, data sovereignty is the idea that nations have the right to exercise authority over data collected within their borders. Just as Alexandria's rulers maintained control over their scrolls, it has now been exchanged for processing units. It is a legal concept that means the data must adhere to the laws and government structures of the country or state in which the data is located or comes from. It is an effort to ensure that the data is treated within local regulations to safeguard privacy rights.

Navigating the intricacies of data sovereignty compliance is pretty much like a journey through complex legal terrain. It frequently demands that organizations allocate substantial resources toward acquiring legal expertise, reinforcing their data infrastructure, and establishing comprehensive compliance protocols to stay abreast of constantly evolving regulations. However, even if you don't possess abundant resources, it's crucial to remain aware of key considerations as you move forward. By arming yourself with knowledge, you empower yourself to avoid potential pitfalls and legal complications down the road (Figure 10.1).

Then there are data localization requirements; think of them as rules that might insist on storing data in specific places. These rules can, at times, cause what is called data fragmentation.[2] It is like a big puzzle broken into countless pieces and scattered all over the place. This fragmentation can make the efficient management and access of data a real challenge, especially for large international companies. It is a bit like trying

FIGURE 10.1   What does data sovereignty look like in action?

to complete that jigsaw puzzle when some of the pieces are missing from a house or have been lost down the back of your sofa.

However, the real complexity arises when data sovereignty intersects with privacy rights. Governments may demand access to private data, and this can create ethical dilemmas. As a result, the management of data sovereignty can disrupt the smooth operation of global businesses, prompting organizations to make changes to how they store and process data. Missteps in this process can have serious legal consequences, including fines, sanctions, and potential legal disputes.

For example, Moscow[3] employs data localization laws to exert control and influence over various foreign entities, such as the Jewish Agency for Israel. In this instance, the Russian government accused the organization of violating privacy regulations by storing Russian citizens' data outside of Russia. This utilization of data laws is part of a broader strategy aimed at managing information, suppressing dissent, and consolidating power in both the digital and offline domains. Russia's approach involves deploying ambiguous speech laws, issuing threats, and imposing fines on tech giants and other organizations, thereby extending its authority into cyberspace and impacting foreign entities operating within its borders and beyond.

In this salsa dance of data governance, it's essential not to forget the backstage security measures. Focusing solely on data sovereignty might unintentionally overlook the critical role of cybersecurity. This leaves data vulnerable to breaches, which is like securing the front entrance while leaving the back door wide open.

Additionally, data sovereignty often intertwines with international relations and trade disputes, playing a significant role in shaping the flow of data across borders. It is a bit like a digital international soap opera, and data is the central character; the storyline is how it acts with its neighbors when it crosses borders; and with any good soap opera, there is always drama.

Now, nations similarly aim to protect their cultural heritage and sensitive information. For instance, France[4] has implemented strict data protection laws to preserve its language and culture, ensuring that data generated within its borders remains under its jurisdiction.

The struggle for data sovereignty is not merely a theoretical concept. It has played out on the global stage with real-world implications. One notable case is the conflict between the United States and the European Union over the transfer of personal data. The EU has been concerned about the privacy of its citizens and has imposed stringent data protection regulations, such as the GDPR, which we spoke about in the last chapter. These regulations aim to ensure that European data remains secure and under European control.

As we navigate the landscape of data sovereignty, finding a balance between the free flow of information and protecting national interests remains a significant challenge. In a world where data is the new oil and information is power, data sovereignty is the key to preserving a nation's digital autonomy.

Data sovereignty has become a paramount concern for our leaders. Understanding what it is, why it matters, and how to navigate it is essential if you are ever thinking of how to scale up your open data activities.

What can it look like in action? GAIA-X[5] is a European initiative that looks to create a secure and interconnected data infrastructure to promote data sovereignty, trustworthiness, and collaboration across the continent. It operates as a digital ecosystem with a core mission: to facilitate the secure sharing and storage of data, all while respecting defined rules and guidelines. This approach lays the groundwork for the accessibility of data and services.

At its core, GAIA-X is a collaborative project between European countries, companies, and organizations that are working together to build a secure and federated data infrastructure. It is driven by a collective desire to reduce Europe's dependence on non-European cloud providers and to enhance the continent's data independence.

It emphasizes the importance of data sharing for businesses, public services, and society as a whole. GAIA-X fosters collaboration among stakeholders, driving discussions on the added value of data sharing, both in terms of business objectives and broader societal benefits.

In the simplest of terms, GAIA-X is a thriving network of cloud service providers, data service providers, and organizations, all united by a shared commitment to a common cause. This case centers on the creation of a fortified, dependable, and seamlessly interconnected data ecosystem within the European landscape. Providers align their services and practices with these guiding principles. Their aim? To furnish users with a sanctuary—a secure and compliant haven where data can be managed, stored, and exchanged with confidence.

Stakeholders involved in GAIA-X sign up to these core principles:[6]

Data Control: You should have the final say over what happens with your data. It's about giving you the power to decide who can use your information.

Trustworthiness: Your data should be handled with the utmost care. Think of it as a guarantee that your data is safe, secure, and used in the right way.

Compatibility: This principle ensures that different tech systems can work together smoothly. It's like making sure all your gadgets can talk to each other without any problems.

Transparency: Being clear and honest about how data is managed is essential. This way, you'll always know what's happening with your information.

Openness: Collaboration and sharing are encouraged. It's like a big team effort where everyone can contribute ideas and solutions.

Data Portability: Imagine your data is like a suitcase you can take anywhere. You should be able to move it between services or platforms easily.

Compliance: This principle means that everyone involved follows the same rules. It's particularly important when it comes to protecting your privacy and your data.

As open data activists, we can all agree this is a step in the right direction, but we must have a say in initiatives like this, and how do we connect to them? Let's face it, if you are starting your journey into open data and you are only thinking small, the GAIA-X framework might seem a bit imposing, but grassroots NGOs and local governments can learn a lot from the initiative.

So, what can we learn from GAIA-X? Here are 5 points aimed at our level of thinking:

CONTROL YOUR DATA

GAIA-X says you should have control over your data. For grassroots organizations, it means making sure you decide what happens to the data you collect.
Application: Tell people how you'll use their data and keep it safe.

KEEP DATA TRUSTWORTHY AND SECURE

GAIA-X wants data to be trustworthy and secure. For grassroots groups, it means making sure your data is safe from harm.
Application: Use safe methods to store and protect data, like locking it away in a secure place.

MAKE DATA WORK TOGETHER

GAIA-X likes it when people are open and honest about data. For grassroots groups, it means telling everyone where your data comes from and how you use it.
Application: Share how you collect data and have open conversations about it with your community.

FOLLOW THE RULES AND LET DATA MOVE

GAIA-X says we should follow rules about data and let people move their data. For grassroots groups, it means obeying local data laws and letting people take their data with them.
Application: Learn the data rules in your area and let people move their data if they want to.

WHAT DOES DATA SOVEREIGNTY LOOK LIKE IN PRACTICE FOR THE THIRD SECTOR?

You need to be mindful of the laws of the country you live in. As we have pointed out, naturally, different nations have different laws they need to abide by. But let us put it into context from a charity perspective.

Let's say you are working on a funding application with a project in two different countries. As part of that, there is a feasibility study you would like to conduct running workshops from. From that data you will use it to form the application evidence for the grant, but you would also like to create a dataset from that to release as open data. How will the prospect of data sovereignty affect you?

So first, you should now grasp that data from different regions has different legal compliance rules you will need to adhere to; ignoring these rules could leave you with a fine; so do your homework; there are chapters in this book that can help you with that.

Following that, you need to make what is called an "adequacy decision"[7] regarding the country you are sending it to. This will be evident that you have determined that the nation has an adequate level of data protection, and you have made an informed decision. You can trust them with the data provided.

When it comes to moving data around, keep it simple: only share what's truly needed for the task at hand and avoid overloading with unnecessary information. Data minimization[8] is about efficiency and privacy, as this is the process where you limit the collection of personal information—be clear and realistic about the type of data you will be sharing with your international partners. Obviously, personal data and any type of data that identifies people face much stricter regulations, but considering this scenario, we want to make this open data. You should not have any of this in the dataset, but just for informative purposes, we need to consider this.

To protect yourself and your data, and of course, you should consider inserting Standard Contractual Clauses (SSCs)[9] in a document between you and your partner, this is essentially a trust document between two organizations that they will act ethically with the data you are sending to them. These agreements lay out clear rules and promises about how your information should be handled, no matter where it goes. Think of SCCs as the "data safety net" that ensures your data is in good hands, even when it travels to places with different privacy rules.

This document is called a "Data Processing Agreement" or a "Data Transfer Agreement."

The name of what it is called may vary, but the SCCs are a crucial component of such agreements when international data transfers are involved.

Here is a basic version you can use as a reference point to write up yourself; just name the document accordingly.

STANDARD CONTRACTUAL CLAUSES FOR DATA TRANSFER DOCUMENT

PARTIES

Data Exporter: [Your Organization's Name and Address]
Data Importer: [Recipient Organization's Name and Address]

DEFINITIONS

"Data Subjects"—People whose data is being transferred.
"Personal Data" —Any information about an identified or identifiable individual, as defined by data protection laws.

BACKGROUND

We, the Data Exporter and Data Importer, intend to create an agreement to ensure the secure transfer of Personal Data.

CLAUSE 1: DATA TRANSFER

1.1.   We are transferring Personal Data to the Data Importer based on the specific data transfer arrangement we've agreed upon in [your specific agreement, contract, or purpose].

CLAUSE 2: DATA IMPORTER'S RESPONSIBILITIES

2.1.   The Data Importer agrees to use the Personal Data only for the purposes we've defined and in compliance with all applicable data protection laws.

2.2.   The Data Importer also commits to putting in place the necessary security measures to protect Personal Data from unauthorized access, disclosure, alteration, or loss.

2.3.   Furthermore, the Data Importer agrees to provide us, upon request, with information about how they handle the data and their compliance with this agreement.

CLAUSE 3: DATA SUBJECT RIGHTS

3.1.   The Data Importer agrees to assist us in responding to requests from Data Subjects who wish to exercise their rights under data protection laws. This includes rights like access, correction, deletion, and objection.

CLAUSE 4: SECURITY

4.1.   The Data Importer commits to taking reasonable steps to ensure that Personal Data remains secure during its transfer, storage, and processing.

CLAUSE 5: SUBPROCESSING

5.1.   The Data Importer will not engage other processors (sub-processors) to handle the data unless we give our written consent.

CLAUSE 6: DATA PROTECTION IMPACT ASSESSMENT (DPIA) AND AUTHORITIES' INVOLVEMENT

6.1.   The Data Importer agrees to collaborate with us on Data Protection Impact Assessments (DPIAs) when necessary according to data protection laws.

6.2.   Additionally, the Data Importer agrees to cooperate with us in informing and consulting with relevant data protection authorities, as required by the law.

CLAUSE 7: RETURNING OR DELETING DATA

7.1.   Upon the end of our data transfer arrangement or our request, the Data Importer will either return the Personal Data to us or securely delete it.

CLAUSE 8: GOVERNING LAW AND JURISDICTION

8.1.   This agreement follows the laws of [Jurisdiction] and any disputes will be resolved exclusively in the courts of [Jurisdiction].

CLAUSE 9: EFFECT OF THE CLAUSES

9.1.   These SCCs are an essential part of our data transfer arrangement and take precedence over any conflicting terms in the agreement.

IN WITNESS WHEREOF,
The parties have signed this agreement on the date mentioned below.
Data Exporter: [Signature]
Data Importer: [Signature]
[Date]
Remember, this template is meant as a starting point. Customize it according to your unique situation and legal requirements, and seek legal counsel to ensure compliance with data protection laws in your jurisdiction.

To sum it up, data sovereignty isn't just a fleeting phenomenon; it's a constant presence in our ever more interconnected global landscape. As data continues to embed itself into our daily routines, the imperative to maintain authority over it remains. Nonetheless, our task is to navigate this terrain with care, seeking equilibrium that encourages global cooperation while reducing impediments.

NOTES

1   Phillips, H. (2010). Great Library of Alexandria. *Library Philosophy and Practice*, Aug. https://nbn-resolving.org/urn:nbn:de:0168-ssoar-190807
2   Kaczmarczyk, M., Barczynski, M., Kilian, W., & Dubnicki, C. (2012, June). Reducing impact of data fragmentation caused by in-line deduplication. In *Proceedings of the 5th Annual International Systems and Storage Conference* (pp. 1–12).
3   Sherman, J. (2022). Russia Is Weaponizing Its Data Laws against Foreign Organizations. *Brookings*.
4   Hélot, C., & Young, A. (2005). The notion of diversity in language education: Policy and practice at primary level in France. *Language, Culture and Curriculum*, 18(3), 242–257.
5   Gaia-X. (n.d.). About Gaia-X. https://gaia-x.eu/what-is-gaia-x/about-gaia-x/
6   Bonfiglio, F. (2021, December 16). Vision & Strategy. *Gaia-X*. https://gaia-x.eu/wp-content/uploads/2021/12/Vision-Strategy.pdf
7   General Publications. (2023, July 10). Adequacy Decision for the EU-US Data Privacy Framework. European Commission. https://commission.europa.eu/document/fa09cbad-dd7d-4684-ae60-be03fcb0fddf_en

8 European Data Protection Supervisor. (n.d.). Data Minimization. https://edps.europa.eu/data-protection/data-protection/glossary/d_en#:~:text=Data%20minimization,necessary%20to%20fulfil%20that%20purpose

9 European Commission. (n.d.). Standard Contractual Clauses (SCC). https://commission.europa.eu/law/law-topic/data-protection/international-dimension-data-protection/standard-contractual-clauses-scc_en

Collective Power

Democratizing Open Data and Overcoming Barriers

11

If you have ever negotiated a working project that relies on labor, you may have encountered the term "collective bargaining chip."

Collective bargaining is a fundamental strategy frequently wielded by trade unions in their efforts to champion the rights and interests of the workforce they represent. At the heart of this process lies a negotiation between unions and employers, with the overarching goal of enhancing working conditions, wage structures, or employee benefits.

In these negotiations, trade unions often deploy an array of tactics. One of the most potent tools in their arsenal is the threat of a strike—a powerful gesture that can halt business operations and demand immediate attention. Additionally, unions may choose the path of compromise, demonstrating a willingness to adjust certain demands in exchange for concessions from employers.

This delicate dance between unions and employers is a testament to the art of negotiation. It's a process where both sides aim to bridge the divide, ultimately forging agreements that serve the best interests of both the dedicated workforce and the employers who rely on their contributions. It's a high-stakes, yet essential, aspect of labor relations that shapes the landscape of modern workplaces.

Expanding our perspective beyond labor unions, the concept of a collective bargaining chip finds application in a multitude of scenarios spanning business, international diplomacy, politics, and community partnerships. At its core, it embodies the profound strength that unity and collective action yield, enabling groups to realize their objectives more effectively than isolated individuals ever could.

At its core, this term encapsulates a strategic asset, resource, or advantage shared by a collective of individuals or entities. This collective possession is a potent instrument wielded to exert influence in negotiations or discussions. It symbolizes something of substantial value that can be offered or traded to sway the course of a specific situation, commonly within the context of negotiations, agreements, or transactions.

DOI: 10.1201/9781032724645-11

As it revolves around the democratic concept of influencing decisions, civil society organizations can employ this approach to collaborate and develop a collective plan of action.

In the context of open data, the concept of a "collective bargaining chip" takes on a dynamic meaning, representing a strategic approach where diverse stakeholders, including government entities, businesses, nonprofit organizations, and the community, unite their data resources for mutual benefit. Instead of guarding their data silos, these entities collaborate to achieve common objectives. This approach underscores the idea that when data providers combine their efforts, they can unlock significantly more value and collectively address shared challenges.

The essence of the collective bargaining approach lies in recognizing the strength that arises from unity. By forming robust alliances and networks, civil society organizations can wield a potent bargaining tool during negotiations with data providers, whether they are government bodies or private corporations. Within these coalitions, communities gain the capacity to advocate for the release of specific datasets crucial to addressing urgent community concerns. They can negotiate for data formats designed to be user-friendly and accessible to individuals of all technical backgrounds. Furthermore, they ensure that the released data aligns with fundamental principles such as transparency, inclusivity, and active community engagement. Additionally, these coalitions hold data providers accountable for safeguarding individual privacy and preventing any misuse of data.

This collective endeavor significantly amplifies the influence of community voices when shaping data policies, making certain that data serves the greater good. By uniting under the banner of collective bargaining, these alliances empower civil society organizations and communities, enabling them to effectively challenge traditional data hierarchies and advocate for a more inclusive, equitable, and community-centric data landscape.

Coming together as a community is a powerful catalyst in the journey to democratize open data and encourage data providers to prioritize accessibility and comprehensibility. When individuals and organizations agree on a shared purpose, their collective strength becomes a driving force for change. By emphasizing the significance of making open data understandable, communities send a resounding message to data providers: transparency should not be an empty promise but a tangible commitment.

Through community-driven initiatives, such as data literacy programs, public awareness campaigns, and collaborative advocacy efforts, this message is consistently reinforced. Open data should not be confined to experts or buried in technocratic hyperbole it should be a resource that empowers everyone. As communities become more informed about the value of open data in addressing local challenges, they gain influence in pushing data providers to adopt practices that prioritize clarity and accessibility. This collective action propels a shift in the data landscape, compelling providers to take the task of making open data understandable seriously, ensuring it truly serves as a tool for societal progress and inclusivity.

Transparency, a cornerstone of democratizing open data, mandates that governments and institutions not only make data easily accessible but also comprehensible to the general public. Open data's essence should never remain hidden behind layers of bureaucratic jargon or technical complexity.

Inclusivity, another vital facet, underscores the importance of considering every voice in the data realm that profoundly affects society. Inclusivity dictates that the perspectives of all communities, particularly historically marginalized ones, must be taken into account when making data-related decisions.

Community engagement represents a pivotal element in democratizing open data. It posits that communities should actively interact with data, ask questions, and provide feedback. This engagement fosters a sense of ownership and shared responsibility, ultimately leading to decisions that are more informed and community-driven.

While open data champions transparency, it must also respect individuals' privacy rights. Data privacy is an integral component of this paradigm, emphasizing the need to anonymize and safeguard data to prevent any harm to individuals or communities arising from its usage. These four principles collectively form the framework for a more equitable, inclusive, and community-centric approach to open data.

The formation of coalitions around open data initiatives holds immense significance in the quest for a more inclusive and democratized data landscape. These alliances serve as powerful mechanisms through which communities collectively advance their interests and shape data policies impacting their lives.

First and foremost, these coalitions become formidable advocates for the release of specific datasets crucial for addressing pressing community issues. By uniting, communities amplify their voices, increasing the likelihood that data providers, whether governmental or private, will prioritize the release of data capable of driving positive change.

These alliances empower communities to champion user-friendly data formats accessible to everyone, regardless of technical expertise. This inclusivity ensures data benefits the entire community, fostering greater engagement and participation.

Additionally, the coalitions play a pivotal role in ensuring that the released data aligns with the fundamental principles of transparency, inclusivity, and community engagement. Through collective advocacy, communities hold data providers accountable for ethical data practices, safeguarding individual privacy, and preventing the potential misuse of sensitive information. These coalitions act as the driving force behind the democratization of open data, ensuring that data serves the greater good and remains a tool for positive societal change.

There is strength in numbers. When civil society organizations come together, their collective voice becomes more influential, increasing the likelihood that data providers will listen to their needs.

Collaborative coalitions empower communities to negotiate for data formats that are not only user-friendly but also accessible to all, regardless of technical expertise. This inclusivity ensures that data doesn't remain confined to a select few but becomes a resource that benefits the entire community, fostering greater engagement and participation.

In essence, these coalitions act as guardians of data integrity and champions of equitable access. They harness the collective strength of civil society organizations to reshape the data landscape, ensuring that data serves as a tool for the greater good and remains a catalyst for positive societal change.

But hey, it is all well and good to talk about this, but how do you put this into practice, and most importantly, how do you bring people to the cause? From experience, creating initiatives like this is to showcase that you are organized and in a position to lead—here is a step-by-step guide that you can use to bring people together and convince them to create a unified approach to open data.

Step 1: Identify Key Stakeholders

Begin by identifying potential stakeholders who have a vested interest in open data initiatives. These may include government entities, businesses, nonprofit organizations, community groups, and data providers.

Step 2: Conduct a Stakeholder Analysis

Understand the motivations, needs, and concerns of each stakeholder group. What benefits do they seek from open data initiatives? What challenges do they face?

Step 3: Define Common Objectives

Highlight the shared goals and benefits of forming a coalition. Emphasize the potential positive impact on data transparency, accessibility, and community engagement.

Step 4: Craft a Compelling Vision

Develop a clear and inspiring vision statement that illustrates the collective power of the coalition. Describe how it can transform the open data landscape for the better, and be really specific to your local area and its needs.

Step 5: Build a Case for Collaboration

Create a persuasive argument for collaboration, emphasizing the strength that unity brings. Point out that collective action can achieve more significant results than individual efforts.

Step 6: Emphasize the Four Principles

Stress the importance of transparency, inclusivity, community engagement, and data privacy as guiding principles for the coalition's actions.

Step 7: Organize Stakeholder Meetings

Arrange meetings or workshops with potential stakeholders to present your vision, case for collaboration, and success stories. Encourage open discussions.

Step 8: Address Concerns and Objections

Be prepared to address any concerns or objections raised by stakeholders. Provide solutions and evidence to alleviate doubts.

Step 9: Develop a Collaboration Framework

Outline the structure, governance, and decision-making processes for the coalition. Define roles and responsibilities for participating organizations.

Step 10: Establish Clear Benefits

Highlight the benefits that stakeholders can gain from joining the coalition, such as increased influence over data policies, access to valuable datasets, and enhanced community engagement.

Step 11: Offer Incentives

Consider offering incentives or perks for coalition members to encourage participation. These could include access to exclusive resources or training opportunities.

Step 12: Create a Memorandum of Understanding (MOU)

Draft an MOU that formalizes the commitment of coalition members. This document should outline shared objectives, responsibilities, and expectations.

This is a formal, written agreement between two or more parties that outlines their mutual goals, commitments, and intentions. In the context of forming a coalition for open data initiatives, in this instance, an MOU serves as a foundational document that clarifies the roles, responsibilities, and expectations of each participating organization or stakeholder. It helps ensure that all parties are on the same page and committed to achieving the coalition's objectives.

Here's what an MOU for a coalition focused on open data initiatives might look like:

MEMORANDUM OF UNDERSTANDING (MOU)
FOR AN OPEN DATA COALITION

Date: [Date of Agreement]

PARTIES TO THE MOU

[Name of Organization 1]
[Name of Organization 2]
[Name of Organization 3]
[List all participating organizations and stakeholders]

OBJECTIVE

The parties to this MOU hereby enter into a collaborative partnership to establish and operate an Open Data Coalition. The primary goal of this coalition is to promote transparency, accessibility, and inclusivity in open data initiatives within [Region/Community] by leveraging the collective power and resources of its members.

ROLES AND RESPONSIBILITIES

[Name of Organization 1]:
   [Specify the organization's key responsibilities, contributions, and commitments to the coalition.]
[Name of Organization 2]:
   [Specify the organization's key responsibilities, contributions, and commitments to the coalition.]
[Name of Organization 3]:
   [Specify the organization's key responsibilities, contributions, and commitments to the coalition.]
[Repeat the above section for all participating organizations, clearly outlining their respective roles.]

COLLABORATION FRAMEWORK

1. Governance

The coalition shall operate under a [specify governance structure, e.g., steering committee] responsible for decision-making and coordination.

2. Meetings and Communication

Regular meetings and communication channels shall be established to facilitate collaboration and information sharing.

3. Data Sharing

Coalition members shall agree to share relevant open data resources for the benefit of the coalition's initiatives, subject to applicable data-sharing agreements and legal requirements.

BENEFITS OF MEMBERSHIP

Participating organizations shall enjoy the following benefits as members of the Open Data Coalition:

- Access to shared resources and datasets
- Enhanced influence on data policies and standards
- Opportunities for collaborative projects and initiatives
- Visibility and recognition as champions of open data

CONFIDENTIALITY AND PRIVACY

The coalition members shall uphold the principles of data privacy and confidentiality and take measures to protect sensitive information in accordance with applicable laws and regulations.

DURATION

This MOU shall be effective upon the date of signing and shall remain in force for a period of [specify duration, e.g., two years], unless extended or terminated by mutual agreement.

AMENDMENTS AND TERMINATION

Amendments to this MOU may be made with the mutual consent of the coalition members. Termination of this MOU shall require written notice and agreement by all participating organizations.

SIGNATORIES

For [Name of Organization 1]:
    Signature: _____ Date: _____
For [Name of Organization 2]:
    Signature: _____ Date: _____
[Repeat for all participating organizations]

Step 13: Foster Ongoing Communication

Establish channels for regular communication and collaboration among coalition members. Encourage the sharing of knowledge and resources.

Step 14: Launch the Coalition

Hold an official launch event or announcement to introduce the coalition to the wider community and garner support.

Step 15: Promote Visibility and Impact

Share the coalition's achievements, initiatives, and progress through various channels, including social media, press releases, and newsletters.

Step 16: Measure and Report Progress

Implement metrics to track the coalition's impact on open data initiatives. Regularly report on accomplishments to maintain transparency.

Step 17: Seek Continuous Improvement

Continuously assess the coalition's effectiveness and seek feedback from stakeholders to make necessary improvements.

Step 18: Expand Membership

Encourage additional stakeholders to join the coalition as it grows and evolves.

Step 19: Celebrate Successes

Celebrate milestones and successes via social media and events to reinforce the coalition's value and motivate ongoing collaboration.

As we head out on our mission to democratize open data and bring together valuable resources, it's essential to confront the challenges that stand in our way. These barriers are the roadblocks we must collectively overcome as we navigate the path toward open data collaboration. By tackling these obstacles together and harnessing our collective strength, we can fully unleash the transformative power of open data, ensuring it's accessible, understandable, and ethically utilized for the greater good of all.

If we come to a point where we have frustrations in regards to why we can't get our providers to release data, we need to understand the barriers that may be preventing them.

In March 2021, the UK Government commissioned the "Increasing Access to Data Across the Economy" Report.[1] The report was funded to provide a framework for prioritizing interventions to increase data access from the private and third sectors, aiming to identify potential government actions and key barriers, with the findings offering initial insights into how such interventions could impact economic activity and inform future evidence-based policy development.

Let's delve into what they found regarding the UK findings.

The knowledge gap poses a significant obstacle in the landscape of data sharing, affecting both data providers and potential users. Data providers frequently struggle to fully grasp the multitude of potential applications for their data holdings. This limited awareness inadvertently hinders the dissemination of invaluable insights that could spark positive change. Conversely, data users find themselves entangled in this web of ignorance, grappling with the scope and possibilities inherent in available data resources. This dual knowledge deficit acts as a formidable barrier, impeding the seamless sharing of data and the realization of its vast societal benefits.

The absence of motivation to share data poses a significant hurdle to open data. Numerous data providers hesitate to share or provide access to their valuable data due to apprehensions regarding the associated costs and the substantial efforts required. These concerns are further amplified by uncertainties about recouping these investments from the entities poised to derive benefits from the shared data.

Advocating for the development of standardized frameworks and infrastructure for data sharing can reduce costs and foster inclusivity. Collaborating with governmental bodies and industry stakeholders to establish such frameworks can level the playing field, making it more feasible for smaller organizations within the third sector to engage in data sharing without being overwhelmed by prohibitive expenses. This approach ensures that the third sector can unlock the transformative potential of data while guaranteeing accessibility for all.

Finally, a pervasive lack of public trust regarding the use of personal data, whether by the public or private sector, poses a substantial challenge. This trust deficit adds another layer of complexity to data-sharing efforts. Individuals often hesitate to consent to data collection and sharing due to fears of potential misuse or privacy breaches. Rebuilding and reinforcing this trust is an essential component of fostering successful data-sharing initiatives, especially in sectors where public data is involved.

These are indeed barriers, but they also present opportunities for some of these points:

LACK OF INCENTIVE AND KNOWLEDGE, AND BUILDING OF TRUST

There are two effective approaches to achieve this:

Formally: You can bring together community groups, wider civil society, and data providers, such as local government, to conduct a workshop on the benefits of open data. This workshop should be promoted as an opportunity to explore open data collaboratively, starting from a blank canvas. The aim would be to engage in activities that can provide data providers with evidence of the community's preferences for data release or strategic directions to follow.

All the resources and guidance necessary for this endeavor can be discovered in the final pages of this book.

This serves as a powerful motivation for data providers, as it allows them to showcase their commitment to meeting the community's requirements and how their contributions can genuinely benefit the community.

Informally: Set up monthly meet-ups in a local bar or coffee shop, invite speakers and take time to network, talk about what you would like to see and how you would like it to happen, and hold votes on strategy mechanisms that your local data providers can adopt.

If it were me, I'd recommend you do both: set up a group, give it a name and an informal constitution, and use that as a foundation to build on.

COMMERCIAL, REPUTATIONAL, AND ETHICAL RISKS

If community organizations united as a collective, they could play a pivotal role in ensuring some of the concerns faced by the government when releasing data, offering expertise in data ethics and privacy protection, and ensuring that data-driven initiatives prioritize the well-being of citizens.

You could consider either setting up a steering group with government officers offered a place or encouraging your local government to do it with local civil society around the table. This helps share the load, in a sense, and everybody can air vulnerabilities. There is no quick fix to this, but taking a holistic approach and evidencing there is a need, want, and will to collaborate on open data will go a long way toward addressing this situation.

One of the things you could do using this medium is to co-design a code of ethics. This is a set of specific rules and guidelines that individuals or organizations are committed to following. This code helps in making ethical decisions in various situations. Along with ethical principles and values, there are clearly defined ethical principles and values that guide behavior. These principles often include concepts such as honesty, integrity, transparency, fairness, and respect.

Here is a simple activity you can use as part of a working group to book a room and give it a name. Here is a way to do it by following the steps on this graphic (Figure 11.1)!

As we close this chapter on democratizing open data and the importance of collective efforts, it's evident that our path forward is not without obstacles. However, the potential for positive change is enormous. As a community, when we come together, champion transparency, inclusivity, and data privacy, and form alliances that derive their strength from our unity, we hold the ability to transform the data landscape.

In doing so, we ensure that open data becomes a true force for the common good, an empowering tool for all, and a driving factor for positive societal transformation. So, let's embark on this journey with unwavering determination, for it is through unity that we unlock open data's incredible potential, benefiting everyone in the process.

FIGURE 11.1   Steps you can take to address data ethics in the community.

NOTE

1 Department for Digital, Culture, Media and Sport. (2021). Increasing Access to Data Across the Economy. https://assets.publishing.service.gov.uk/government/uploads/system/uploads/attachment_data/file/974532/Frontier-access_to_data_report-26-03-2021.pdf

Trust in Our Institutions, Does It Affect Digital Strategy?

12

You probably don't need me to inform you that there are significant trust issues between local activists and decision-makers in our towns and cities worldwide. It is crucial to hold politicians accountable for the choices they make, as they shape the policy agenda and our involvement in community services. I understand that this chapter may appear somewhat negative, but to fit into the broader narrative, we must address this matter.

Distrust between civil society organizations and government,[1] particularly at the local level, is not news for those of us working in these sectors. Drawing from my own experiences, I've been part of government initiatives focused on engaging with communities, collecting valuable insights on digital-related matters like skills, and seeing these projects through to their conclusion for outreach to end after the funding has ceased. Despite the government in question having gathered valuable evidence that could shape policies for the better, the community often perceives it as though the local authority simply got what it wanted and then lost interest. While this perception may not align with reality, it's easy to understand why such sentiments persist.

This is very impactful because these conversations are frequent between third-sector workers. Also, government workers from different departments will be well aware of the issue of working in silos within their own work; this has a ripple effect on how they communicate projects that can span different departments. It becomes more challenging to devise a cohesive strategy to communicate the project's outcomes, the utilization of data, and how to access the findings (Figure 12.1).

However, does this distrust go beyond the typical relational attitude between these two counterparts? I believe it does. While I can only provide feedback from a British and personal working perspective internationally, I know there are similarities between my work and conversations I've had with other activists and professionals across Europe, and beyond.

Sometimes, it is a matter of social culture and a lack of confidence in our systems. Grassroots NGOs frequently exhibit mistrust towards the government, particularly their local government authorities.[2]

DOI: 10.1201/9781032724645-12

FIGURE 12.1 Building trust with open data can be a bit like Lego.

But is the notion of mistrusting our leaders deeply ingrained? Is it culturally embedded within us to distrust decision-makers, and does this spill over into grassroots relationships that our overburdened civil servants must manage?

"I think the people of this country have had enough of experts"[3] famously declared a British politician during the turbulent Brexit referendum campaign, which resulted in the country narrowly voting to leave the European Union. This statement literally divided the nation.

Surprisingly, the rhetoric from the Vote Leave side resonated more than one would expect from a British perspective. The notion of individualism is deeply rooted in English society,[4] giving people a sense that they know what is best for their lives rather than relying on experts. The idea of some out-of-touch scientist or academic dictating how to think and live is met with resistance.

The politician tapped into the growing anti-intellectualism[5] that permeates our global society. Many political campaigns worldwide have been based on this sentiment over the past couple of decades, unfortunately.

Campaign after campaign has adopted an anti-intellectual stance, and regrettably, it has been effective. From the chorus of "drain the swamp"[6] in America, Viktor Orbán's strange confrontation with philanthropist George Soros,[7] which included state-funded media campaigns to vilify Soros and the revival of ancient anti-Semitic stereotypes, to former Brazilian premier Jair Bolsonaro's initial 2 months in office dedicated to dismantling the education ministry, including threats to send troops into public schools to eradicate any references to the 1964 coup[8] and the subsequent 21 years of military rule.

But what does all this have to do with open data?

Well, if we amplify the existing strained trust relationship, particularly when local authorities genuinely strive to accomplish their tasks, it further complicates their already challenging job. It has a knock-on effect.

And let's be honest, open data is already incredibly challenging to communicate to those who are not already aware. It is often considered the epitome of hard-to-reach policy.

As the political landscape evolves and disdain for the political establishment grows worldwide, digital activists using open data can be a means to measure the impact of our local elected officials' work and a way to monitor whether they are fulfilling their promises. Open data is just one of the tools at our disposal to craft a debate based on facts in the face of resistance to evidence.

To the general public, terms such as open data, smart cities, digital democracy, civic technology, and open-source platforms mean very little. They might wonder if these are just more "experts" talking about things they don't understand or if there is substance to them.

Unfortunately, many technological outlooks have been associated with negative political rhetoric, especially in the UK. I distinctly recall a former leader of a major political party in the UK discussing the importance of digital democracy,[9] only to be criticized in the press. I was disheartened when I watched a lunchtime political program where the presenter dismissed his ideas as nonsense, not even a panelist, but the presenter. Digital democracy is a remarkable concept, and, unfortunately, some people's first encounter with it was tainted by political biases.

We need to look at where this has been done right, and when it comes to digital democracy, it's the glitzy heights of what you would think when it comes to the tech world. It is a tiny Baltic nation with a population of under 1.5 million.

Estonia's achievement[10] in using digital democracy and establishing trust can be credited to its forward-thinking approach and unwavering commitment to e-governance. By implementing robust cybersecurity measures, safeguarding privacy, ensuring transparency, and facilitating government services' accessibility, Estonia succeeded in fostering a profound trust within its citizenry.

They wholeheartedly embraced the internet as an indispensable tool for democratic participation, propelling Estonia out of poverty and positioning it as an exemplar of contemporary democratic governance. 99% of Estonian governance is online.[11] From voting to trash collection, one of the only things citizens would need to leave the house for that they could not do online is getting a divorce.

In 2023, I visited Tallinn to attend the Open Government Partnership Summit. There, I watched Estonian Prime Minister Kaja Kallas's opening speech, in which she said, "our government vision is clear, a world where governments act in partnership with the civil society and the people." And they are really backing this up with action, creating a whole open-source toolkit on the paths other nations can follow their digitalization roadmap, called X-Road.[12] Governments from across the world can put this into practice simply by visiting a website and downloading the tools they need. To me, that is revolutionary to global government transparency.

And the proof is in the pudding; in regards to building trust, research from the University of Oxford—Oxford Internet Institute in their report *It's Not Only Size That*

Matters: Trust and E-Government Success in Europe states "Trust is an important factor in e-government success, and Estonia's high level of trust in its government is likely one of the reasons for its success in e-government."[13]

Back in the UK, for digital activists aiming to encourage NGOs to embrace digital tools for capacity building, the negative portrayal of digitalization in the media can be disheartening. It often leads to the public's first exposure to the term being through journalists criticizing politicians on television, which has a negative connotation, regardless of the accuracy of their statements. This not only shapes public opinion but also influences how individuals perceive the politicians in question, not the actual subject.

For citizens who aren't directly involved in the field or have an interest in open government, these concepts mean very little. However, it's crucial for the community to recognize that there is something that can amplify their voices and empower them to influence local governance.

Before policymakers propose digital initiatives that will impact people's lives, they must invest time and resources in educating the public about future technologies. Otherwise, it becomes a futile endeavor that undermines the valuable work of activists and organizations in addressing the digital divide and supporting charities and voluntary groups.

Local governments are seen in most places as your first port to open data, leading these institutions to collaborate with universities, innovation laboratories, and large corporations to shape their outreach mechanisms without really considering community representation on a wider scale. It is important to involve major players when developing a new digital approach, but neglecting community infrastructure representation can result in poor policy outreach and challenges to the legitimacy of decision-making processes.

Engaging community entities requires careful consideration and cannot be approached casually. Grassroots NGOs consist of ordinary people, not political scientists, so the narrative must be relatable and easily understood; it is not rocket science.

Imagine being a local volunteer working with a community-based organization and attending a workshop where a community outreach officer from the local municipality discusses upcoming strategies using complex terms such as IoT, blockchains, or smart cities. It would likely create confusion and dissatisfaction. By taking this approach, grassroots organizations will disengage, further eroding the already fragile trust between local government and the third sector.

Repairing damaged relationships incurs significant costs in terms of time and money. It often requires the intervention of professionals to rebuild trust and design outreach projects to involve community groups. This not only becomes expensive but also reflects poorly on government efforts—and I say this from experience because—for a long time, this is how I paid the bills.

While it may sound pessimistic, assuming that organizations may have trust issues and using that as a basis for communication can help appreciate the need for clear and accessible language. If you can't explain a concept to a random person on the street, it is unlikely to make sense to a community activist.

Plus, third-sector organizations serve diverse and specialized demographics in hyperlocal settings. They cater to various cultural and ethnic groups, providing inclusive social support systems. Ignoring these organizations because they don't fit the typical outreach profile is not acceptable. Outreach strategies aimed at enhancing the digital capacity of the third sector should inform them about open data, its importance, and how it can benefit the people they serve.

Not only are charity, civil, and voluntary organizations struggling to understand the rhetoric around open data, but even some coworkers in local government face similar challenges. Senior staff members, hesitant to appear uninformed about new initiatives, may not voice their concerns. I have witnessed this firsthand, where very senior employees responsible for open data projects lack a clear understanding and struggle to explain their purpose.

This isn't the fault of government officers, but a result of their interactions and exposure to a technocratic culture. Often, smart city agendas are set by external agencies commissioned by a central government, who swoop in with glossy marketing material, expensive suits, and buzzword-filled presentations. This top-down approach can easily influence participants, as local government leaders sign up for it, giving the impression that decisions have already been made.

If that is the culture, can you expect government workers to be confident enough to come forward and ask for further training or admit that they don't understand certain digital policy mechanisms?

Usually, after these activities, they go to a "commissioning group," which is a steering group of local leaders and actors that meets monthly to identify opportunities, investments, or funding potential in that local government catchment area and then formulate methods to facilitate that.

These meetings can be quite hectic, and to be honest, they create a highly competitive environment. Sometimes, people around these tables want to be heard and seen, feeling the need to justify their presence or position at these tables. In my opinion, this kind of culture is not conducive to good strategy.

From a community developer's point of view, when you run workshops in the community, you have to manage the louder voices in the room to gather a real consensus. In the settings mentioned above, you need a strong chair to do that. However, it is harder because every single person around that table who is not from the government sector clamors over each other to prove that they have the right to be there.

Personally, I have sat on various steering groups like these within different UK authorities, especially in the earlier days of working on the smart cities agenda. I can honestly say that I was confused by the language that was thrown around the table, and I'll admit that I found it intimidating to the point where I struggled to engage. I kept telling myself, "I should know all this; I have to work harder."

I studied and studied until I reached a point where I was more confident and participated in more debates. After a while, I started to realize that most of the people around the table were just as clueless as me, and the conversations were mostly just a competition for filibustering, like a middle-class and middle-aged rap battle.

This made me think: if I find this confusing and can't comprehend why, as a group, we lean towards overcomplicating our language, how can we expect community groups to understand the premise of the project when there is already an overwhelming need for digital training within the third sector?

It seems that some governments have a methodological bias when it comes to approaching innovation.

It is essential to bridge the gap between policymakers and the community by using clear and relatable language, involving community representatives in decision-making processes, and educating both the public and government employees about the benefits and relevance of open data. Only then can we establish trust, enhance civic engagement, and effectively leverage digital tools for positive change in society.

There is a slight difference in influencing research between central governments and large city governments compared to smaller municipalities when implementing digital outreach.

You could argue that it's about skill sets, but money also plays a significant role. Smaller areas may not have the luxury of launching outreach programs and funding opportunities, but they still have similar digital priorities. When these smaller authorities start researching strategies, they look to their larger city counterparts for inspiration. However, critical thinking becomes imperative. We have to ask ourselves: Is this right for us? Would this type of narrative or activity gain traction in our communities or simply cause more problems in the long run? Such as the Sandwell example I lay out in the "Making Open Data Outreach Human Centred" chapter.

However, I believe that more marginalized areas can create their own exemplary projects and have these high-income areas look to them for community outreach on digital policy rights. Their biggest resource is people, and they have a strong community-based ecosystem thriving with neighborhood assets such as hyperlocal NGOs, small businesses, community centers, civic groups, health initiatives, and of course, residents who genuinely depend on each other to exist. So, let's include them.

The point I'm trying to make is that we should learn from each other because it's never a one-way relationship, especially in community development. And we have to take that path with our outreach strategy if we want to have any substance with the people we are trying to support.

When digital policy is written, usually other departments are responsible for implementing outreach. In the case of digital or ICT policy, the strategy is created by those departments, and community development officers are usually tasked with carrying out outreach-related activities. This means that less digitally savvy officers are usually responsible for facilitating it.

Consistently, frontline public servants do not receive the protection they deserve from their managerial teams. Working for a local authority is quite institutionalized, and there is a sense of competition among the various divisions. As a result, entire teams often work independently without exchanging information.

This has affected the confidence of staff members when it comes to explaining digital-related issues and could lead to third-sector organizations disengaging or sometimes affecting that fragile trust because community members don't understand the language, as we discussed earlier in this book. Simply put, more work needs to be done to ensure that frontline staff have all the tools they need to ensure policy outcomes are met.

Regardless of whether it's open data or digital government issues, this has caused significant problems in the past when it comes to relationship breakdowns between local governments and neighborhoods.

The thing is, policymakers don't always consider in-house skills issues when forming a strategy. It's not as obvious to them, and they feel that it's the responsibility of the department to arrange training and upskilling to align with wider government strategy, especially within local government. They are too busy with the subject at hand and the various partners involved in helping them shape the content.

To address this issue, I conducted a series of rapid prototyping workshops with nine governments across five continents. The goal was to help them develop localized descriptions that every department can refer to when explaining open data. We recommended creating an elevator pitch formulated by ICT departments and policymakers that could be shared with frontline staff so they feel more confident when interacting with community stakeholders. We also suggested including follow-up questions, as it is a cost-effective approach.

When we asked participants why they thought this was important, they stated:

- It ensures a cohesive message.
- It prevents deviation from the narrative set by policymakers when informing about open data and delivering or identifying community-based training.
- It promotes more inclusive outreach.
- It helps achieve policy outcomes and provides visible evidence.
- It encourages the use of more open data by smaller grassroots projects.

Moving forward, policymakers need to consider not only policy development but also the skill sets of the people implementing the work on the frontlines. And honestly, it's not difficult to do. It could be as simple as organizing training workshops or providing support packs. Just ensure that those on the frontlines have all the tools they need to make meaningful connections through outreach.

This needs to happen because it can bring together different disciplines. For example, if there is a community event involving training community actors, why wouldn't you tell them about your open data mechanisms if they could help their project and expand its impact? Leaders need to be mindful of this if they truly want to create inclusive outreach.

If you can achieve that and get your communities to engage with you, then other authorities will look to your multiplicity as a model.

Never be afraid to break the mold. Good innovation isn't just about technology or impressive narratives; it's about engagement followed by measurable results. There is a reason why smart city projects have a very short shelf life, and one of the important reasons is limited engagement due to ineffective outreach.

NOTES

1 The Pompidou Group & Council of Europe. (2017). Government Interaction with Civil Society [Policy Paper]. https://rm.coe.int/government-interaction-with-civil-society-policy-paper-on-government-i/168075b9d9

2 Schuller, M. (2012). *Killing with Kindness: Haiti, International Aid, and NGOs*. Rutgers University Press.

3 Portes, R. (2017, May 09). I Think the People of This Country Have Had Enough of Experts. London Business School. https://www.london.edu/think/who-needs-experts

4 White, S. D., & Vann, R. T. (1983). The invention of English individualism: Alan Macfarlane and the modernization of pre-modern England. *Social History*, 8, 345.

5 Motta, M. (2018). The dynamics and political implications of anti-intellectualism in the United States. *American Politics Research*, 46(3), 465–498.

6 Hudson, R. B. (2018). Draining the swamp while making America great again: Senior dissonance in the age of Trump. *Journal of Aging & Social Policy*, 30(3–4), 357-371.

7 Visnovitz, P., & Jenne, E. K. (2021). Populist argumentation in foreign policy: The case of Hungary under Viktor Orbán, 2010–2020. *Comparative European Politics*, 19, 683–702.

8 Giordano, C. (2019, April 4). Brazil Rewrites School Textbooks 'to Deny 1964 Revolution'. *The Independent*. https://www.independent.co.uk/news/world/americas/brazil-revolution-1964-military-coup-textbooks-education-minister-a8855581.html

9 Richards, L. (2016, September 1). Digital Democracy: How Well Does Jeremy Corbyn's Manifesto Bring Social Media and Socialism Together? Search Engine Watch. https://www.searchenginewatch.com/2016/09/01/digital-democracy-how-well-does-jeremy-corbyns-manifesto-bring-social-media-and-socialism-together/

10 Diaz, J. (2021). Towards More 'E-Volved' Democracy: An Exploration of Digital Governance in Estonia and the Lessons It Holds for Strengthening Democracy in the United States. NEXTUKUE Working Paper Series.

11 OECD. (2019). Digital Opportunities for Better Agricultural Policies (Chapter 13). https://www.oecd-ilibrary.org/sites/510a82b5-en/index.html?itemId=/content/component/510a82b5-en#:~:text=However%2C%20a%20few%20indicators%20are,million%20digital%20signatures%20per%20year

12 The Government of the Republic of Estonia. (n.d.). X-Road®. https://e-estonia.com/solutions/interoperability-services/x-road/

13 Stephany, F. (2020). It's Not Only Size That Matters: Trust and E-Government Success in Europe. Available at SSRN 3722293.

Empowering Collaborative Communities

13

The Role of Data-Driven Decision-Making in Promoting Co-Ownership and Shared Responsibility

On 4 November 1854, a young Italian-born English woman arrived on the shores of Istanbul, Turkey, with a team of 54 volunteers to tend to wounded soldiers during the Crimean War at a barracks that had been turned into a hospital.

Amidst the grim backdrop of the war, an unsettling chapter unfolded within the confines of the Selimiye Barracks. The toll of the conflict extended far beyond the battlefield, as approximately 6,000 soldiers met their untimely demise, primarily due to the merciless grip of a cholera epidemic due to poor hygiene and a lack of access to clean water.

Her contributions during the Crimean War left an indelible mark in the field of healthcare. Her emphasis on hygiene, sanitation, and compassionate patient care set new standards for nursing practices.[1] Beyond her immediate impact on the war's medical facilities, her work continued to influence healthcare systems worldwide. Her legacy paved the way for the professionalization of nursing as a respected profession, inspiring countless individuals to follow in her footsteps and dedicate their lives to caring for the sick and injured.

Just 3 years later, this young woman returned home to England as a hero, dragging the profession of nursing into a modern era. Today, her principles[2] remain foundational in modern nursing education and practice, highlighting the enduring significance of her pioneering efforts in the world of healthcare.

DOI: 10.1201/9781032724645-13

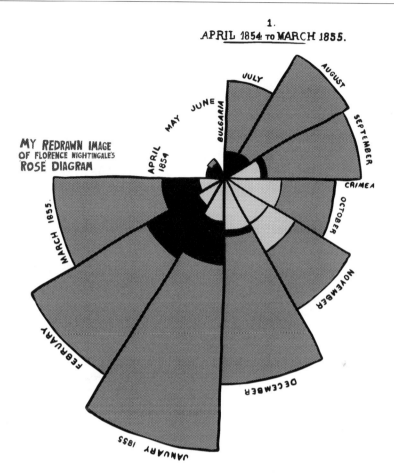

FIGURE 13.1   The diagram that some say started it all.

She also pioneered the idea of data-driven decision-making (DDDM). This remarkable person, otherwise known as the Lady with the Lamp, was Florence Nightingale (Figure 13.1).[3]

She was a fervent advocate for healthcare reform and used the data she collected during the Crimean War, which encompassed mortality rates, disease prevalence, sanitary conditions, nutrition, hospital management, patient records, and environmental factors, to champion improvements in healthcare and hospital practices. It was ultimately her efforts that contributed to the introduction of the British Public Health Act of 1875.

The British Public Health Act of 1875 was a revolutionary piece of legislation that significantly transformed public health practices in the United Kingdom. It established crucial requirements for sanitation, clean water, regulated building codes, and sewer systems. This landmark act laid the foundation for modern public health infrastructure and played a pivotal role in doubling the average human lifespan over the following century. Its impact extended far beyond the UK, serving as a model for public health reforms in many other countries.

Even though the concept of DDDM may seem like a new concept, it is not. The idea of collecting data to influence decisions is quite ancient—very ancient, in fact. It can be traced back to 3800 BCE in the Babylonian Empire,[4] where they collected data on livestock and quantities of butter, honey, milk, wool, and vegetables.

One of the earliest comprehensive censuses was a little bit more recent than that, though.

Initiated in 1381 CE during the Ming Dynasty by Emperor Hongwu, it marked a pivotal moment in the history of systematic data collection. The Yellow Register,[5] conducted periodically, aimed to gather detailed information about the populace, including household sizes, ages, genders, and occupations. The data collected through the Yellow Register played a critical role in shaping significant governmental decisions, such as tax rate determinations and military conscription quotas.

Notably, the Yellow Register stood out as one of the most comprehensive and accurate censuses of its era, positioning it as a valuable historical resource. Historians have heavily relied on its data to gain insights into the Ming Dynasty, enabling in-depth examinations of the dynasty's population dynamics, economic structures, and societal aspects.

Despite its discontinuation in 1644 CE following the collapse of the Ming Dynasty, the legacy of the Yellow Register endures, as it continues to offer a wealth of information for researchers and scholars seeking to understand the intricacies of the Ming Dynasty's history and governance.

So, it is still influencing decisions today, nearly 400 years later.

Now that you know some historical background, let us come back into the 21st century.

DDDM is the process of leveraging data to inform and enhance decision-making processes. This approach involves the systematic collection, analysis, and interpretation of data to uncover trends and patterns that can guide more informed choices.

The significance of DDDM cannot be overstated, as it offers organizations numerous advantages in terms of performance, efficiency, and profitability. By harnessing the power of data, organizations can make well-founded decisions related to their products, services, and marketing campaigns (Figure 13.2).

But what can it mean for the third sector?

Improved Decision-Making for the Third Sector: DDDM empowers organizations within the third sector to enhance their decision-making processes significantly. By harnessing data-driven insights, these organizations can chart a course toward more effective choices, ultimately leading to heightened performance, improved operational efficiency, and increased impact in their communities. Through a systematic analysis of data, third-sector organizations gain a clearer perspective, enabling them to make well-informed decisions that drive positive change.

Risk Reduction and Resilience: The third sector often faces unique challenges, making risk management a critical concern. DDDM serves as a powerful ally in this regard. By proactively utilizing data to identify and mitigate potential risks and challenges, these organizations can safeguard their stability and resilience. For instance, through data analysis, a nonprofit can recognize emerging trends in donor behavior and adjust fundraising strategies accordingly, ensuring sustainable support for its mission.

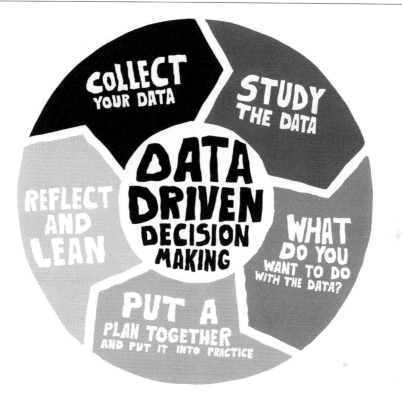

FIGURE 13.2   Data-driven decision-making process.

Enhanced Stakeholder Engagement: Understanding and meeting the diverse needs of stakeholders, including beneficiaries and supporters, is fundamental for third-sector success. DDDM empowers organizations to delve deep into stakeholder preferences and behaviors. By dissecting data, a nonprofit can identify the most impactful programs or services, allocate resources more effectively, and ultimately enhance stakeholder satisfaction. This data-driven approach fosters stronger connections with stakeholders, encouraging ongoing support and collaboration.

Competitive Advantage in the Pursuit of Social Impact: In a landscape where resources are often limited, gaining a competitive edge is crucial for third-sector organizations. DDDM provides nonprofits and community-focused entities with a unique advantage by guiding them toward superior decision-making based on data-driven insights. By examining good data, these organizations can uncover hidden opportunities to maximize their social impact. This proactive approach positions them ahead of the curve, allowing them to address critical community needs more effectively and make a meaningful difference.

How could it have a tangible look? These are some scenarios I have thought up to help you visualize what it can look like.

PROMOTING CORNISH LANGUAGE EDUCATION IN CORNWALL

Scenario: A community group in Cornwall aims to introduce Cornish language lessons into local schools. To support their cause, they conducted extensive surveys in various towns across Cornwall to gauge public interest and gather data on the demand for Cornish language education.

Data-Driven Approach: By analyzing survey results, the community group can identify which towns have the highest demand for Cornish language lessons. Armed with this data, they can organize a presentation for local members of parliament and the county council, showcasing the findings to make a compelling case for the inclusion of Cornish language lessons in the curriculum.

REBUILDING COMMUNITIES IN MOSUL, IRAQ

Scenario: A human rights organization operating in Iraq is focused on aiding displaced people in Mosul. They gather data on the number of displaced individuals, assess the cost of rebuilding properties, and engage with local citizens to determine the preferred path for reconstruction.

Data-Driven Approach: Using data on displacement and reconstruction costs, the organization formulates a data-driven funding proposal targeting international aid agencies. By aligning their proposal with community preferences for reconstruction, they increase the likelihood of securing funding and efficiently aiding the affected population.

COMBATTING HEART DISEASE AND STROKE IN SOMALILAND

Scenario: The Somaliland government collaborates with an in-country health charity to address heart disease and stroke risks. They use data to identify high-risk communities, engage with these communities, and leverage the gathered information to run government-led awareness campaigns.

Data-Driven Approach: The government uses data analysis to pinpoint communities most vulnerable to heart disease and stroke. Armed with this insight, they tailor awareness campaigns to reach the at-risk populations effectively. Data informs campaign strategies and resource allocation, maximizing the impact of their efforts.

Ending Ala Kachuu in Kyrgyzstan

Scenario: A Kyrgyz women's rights organization campaigns to eradicate Ala Kachuu, a form of bride kidnapping still practiced[6] in Kyrgyzstan. They survey victims and individuals who have experienced this practice and present their findings to the Supreme Council.

Data-Driven Approach: By gathering and analyzing data on Ala Kachuu, the organization compiles a comprehensive report for the Supreme Council. This data-driven presentation serves as the basis for policy change. In response, the government decided to enhance education efforts in schools and community centers, addressing the issue more effectively based on the survey findings.

DDDM equips us with the necessary tools to make informed choices, drawing from both publicly available data and data we've gathered firsthand.

Furthermore, it fosters a sense of collective responsibility toward addressing local issues. By immersing ourselves in data and amplifying its insights, we can substantially increase the tangible outcomes of our efforts. Whether it involves exerting public pressure on decision-makers to enact change in our community or crafting agendas that align with the needs of our community members, data forms the foundation of consensus-building. Ultimately, this consensus is based on information generated by the very people we aim to assist, ensuring that our actions are both relevant and impactful.

I'd like to emphasize the remarkable potential that DDDM offers us—the ability to collaboratively design our services, outreach efforts, and social action initiatives alongside our local community. While engaging residents is essential, it also serves as a powerful tool for building positive public relations because it is evidence that we not only listen to the people we support but also openly incorporate their needs into our way of working.

For community-driven codesign, enhancing relevance and effectiveness is paramount.

Active involvement of local residents leads to the creation of services and activities that truly resonate with the community's unique needs, preferences, and challenges. By evaluating the data, we gain invaluable insights that enable us to fine-tune our offerings to directly address these local concerns. This tailored approach results in higher satisfaction and more positive outcomes, making our initiatives not only relevant but profoundly effective.

Trust is the cornerstone of successful community engagement. By designing services with local residents, we take a strategic step toward building trust and fostering stronger community relations. It's not merely a tactic; it's a reflection of our organization's genuine commitment to valuing the voices and perspectives of the community we serve. In essence, it's a testament that we're here to collaborate and serve, rather than impose our solutions. This approach to codesign isn't just about projects; it's about building lasting trust and goodwill.

One of the remarkable outcomes of data-driven codesign is the empowerment it offers local residents. When we involve them in the decision-making process, we're essentially saying, "Your input matters and you have the power to shape your community's future." This empowerment goes beyond project specifics; it sparks increased civic engagement. Community members become active participants in driving positive change, leading to a sense of ownership over the solutions that impact their lives.

While the short-term benefits of codesign are evident, our focus extends to long-term sustainability. Engaging the community in the design process ensures that they become champions of the initiatives we undertake. This sustained support from within the community ensures that projects continue to thrive long after their inception. It's a commitment to creating an enduring impact and ensuring that these endeavors benefit the community for years to come.

So, where is a good place to start? If you are starting from scratch but are interested in how you can bring your community actors together to gather data to influence local policy or decisions based on community needs, here is a short event you can try. You can run this in person, but perhaps it is best suited to an online workshop:

Rapid Fire Workshop: Collective Data Gathering for Informed Decision-Making
Welcome to our rapid-fire online workshop! In just 90 minutes, we'll explore how collective data gathering can influence decisions and create a common pool of insights. Let's dive right in.
Agenda:
Icebreaker (5 minutes):
Start with a quick icebreaker to energize participants and create a lively atmosphere.

Introduction to Collective Data Gathering (10 minutes):
Explain the workshop's purpose: to collectively gather data and understand its influence on decision-making.
Share real-life examples of how data-driven decisions have impacted communities.

Data Gathering Conversations 1: Personal Stories (15 minutes):
Participants take turns sharing personal stories or experiences related to the community issue they are looking to change.
The facilitator encourages discussions, and key points are noted for reference.

Data Gathering Conversations 2: Brainstorming (10 minutes):
Brainstorm common challenges or opportunities based on the shared stories.
Encourage participants to contribute ideas during the conversation.

Data Gathering Conversations 3: Prioritization (5 minutes):
Have participants collectively decide on the most critical challenges or opportunities identified.

Introduction to Data Collection Tools (10 minutes):
Briefly introduce various data collection tools, such as surveys, interviews, and observations.
Explain their relevance in gathering insights.

Data Gathering Conversations 4: Collective Decision (10 minutes):

Engage participants in a discussion to collectively decide on the best data collection method.

Discuss setting up a shared data collection spreadsheet, survey portal, or data collection platform; make sure you collectively choose a tool you can all access and everybody understands; and keep it as simple as you can.

Setting Up Shared Data Collection (10 minutes):

Provide a brief demonstration of how to use the shared data collection spreadsheet or survey.

Discuss the benefits of having a shared method for ongoing data collection.

Data Compilation and Insights (10 minutes):

Explain the importance of collecting and compiling the survey results.

Data-Informed Decision-Making (10 minutes):

Discuss how the collected data can influence decisions and actions of the chosen issue.

Encourage participants to share their thoughts on potential next steps.

Building a Common Pool of Insights (5 minutes):

Emphasize the importance of pooling insights and data as a community resource.

Discuss the collective maintenance of a shared platform or repository for ongoing data collection.

Action Planning (5 minutes):

Have participants identify actionable steps they can take based on the insights gained.

Discuss forming task forces or committees to address specific issues.

Sharing and Closing (5 minutes):

Participants briefly share their takeaways from the workshop and what they hope to achieve with the collective data they will all collect.

Follow-Up (5 minutes):

Put a follow-up meeting in the diary to oversee how it is all going.

LOW-TECH VS HIGH-TECH

Third-sector workers and even those who work in some government agencies, especially at the local level, can sometimes opt for the more cost-effective choice, which is fair enough. However, it's important that we explore both high-tech and low-tech solutions that can assist us in making decisions based on our data.

Low-tech approaches to DDDM are characterized by their reliance on simple tools and techniques. Considering we want the most social impact in our work, this is a section we need to cover. These methods often involve using readily available resources, such as spreadsheets, whiteboards, and manual data collection processes. Low-tech approaches are known for their accessibility and affordability, making them suitable options for organizations with limited resources or technical expertise.

On the other hand, high-tech approaches to DDDM leverage sophisticated tools and techniques such as machine learning, artificial intelligence, and big data analytics. These advanced methods enable organizations to extract powerful insights from their data, facilitating more informed decision-making processes. However, it's important to note that high-tech approaches can come with higher costs and greater complexity in implementation.

In our pursuit of maximum social impact, it's essential to consider both high-tech and low-tech solutions for DDDM. These approaches provide valuable tools for organizations working toward positive change. While low-tech methods offer accessibility and affordability, high-tech solutions unlock advanced insights, ensuring that we can harness the full potential of our data to drive meaningful decisions and outcomes.

Let's explore examples of both low-tech and high-tech approaches in the context of DDDM:

Low-Tech Approaches

Spreadsheet Analysis: Organizations can use spreadsheets to track and analyze data, such as figures or feedback. This low-tech method allows for basic data organization and trend identification.

Activity Feedback From Work Meetings, Events, or Workshops: Collecting feedback from work meetings, events, or workshops can be a valuable practice for gaining insights and improving future initiatives. After gathering this information, it's essential to organize and anonymize it, typically by compiling it into a report or spreadsheet. This process enables you to extract meaningful insights from the data (do not forget to anonymize the data, though), enhancing the quality and effectiveness of upcoming community activities and initiatives.

Surveys and Interviews: Conducting surveys and interviews with customers or stakeholders is a low-tech method for gathering valuable insights and feedback.

Manual Data Collection: Using paper-based forms, checklists, or logs for data collection remains a straightforward way to capture information, especially in situations where technology may not be readily available.

High-Tech Approaches

Machine Learning Predictions: High-tech approaches involve using machine learning algorithms, which can be thought of as digital brains that learn from historical data to predict stakeholder behavior within charities and the third sector. For instance, a charity might use machine learning to forecast donor engagement or volunteer participation.

This technology allows organizations to identify patterns and trends in past interactions, helping them tailor their outreach efforts more effectively. Machine learning is a bit like a digital brain; it learns from the data you provide and offers insights and feedback based on that learning. By understanding the factors that influence stakeholder engagement, charities and third-sector organizations can make data-driven decisions to enhance their community impact and achieve their missions more efficiently.

Predictive Analytics: This is a complex yet invaluable tool that empowers organizations to anticipate future trends based on historical data patterns. It's akin to having a reliable crystal ball for making informed decisions. By meticulously examining extensive datasets and recognizing subtle correlations, predictive analytics provides businesses with a strategic advantage, enabling them to foresee potential opportunities and challenges.

In practical terms, imagine a retailer using predictive analytics to optimize inventory management. By analyzing past sales, seasonal trends, and other relevant factors, the retailer can make accurate forecasts about which products will be in demand in the coming months. This foresight helps prevent overstocking or understocking, ultimately enhancing customer satisfaction and profitability.

Big Data Analytics: High-tech big data analytics processes large datasets to uncover complex patterns and trends. Organizations can gain deeper insights into customer behavior and market dynamics using these tools.

Data Visualization Tools: Utilizing data visualization tools and high-tech approaches enables the creation of interactive dashboards and reports that communicate data-driven insights effectively to stakeholders.

Tip: Various survey applications have a data visualization feature, allowing you to transform your surveyed data into graphs or charts. While they may not always provide a download option, you can take a screenshot, paste it into a word processing document, and easily crop it. Voilà! You now have free data visualization based on the information you've collected, which you can use for reports and share online as evidence of your work.

Selecting the Right Approach

The choice between low-tech and high-tech approaches to DDDM depends on several factors:

Budget: Consider the financial resources available. Low-tech methods are often cost-effective, while high-tech solutions may require substantial investments.

Resources: Assess the technical expertise within your organization. Low-tech approaches may be more accessible for those with limited technical skills.

Specific Needs: Evaluate your organization's data analysis needs. High-tech methods are suited for handling complex data and extracting intricate insights.

Experience: If you are new to DDDM, or if your organization is in the early stages of data utilization, low-tech approaches can provide a simpler starting point.

Hybrid Approach: Combining low-tech and high-tech methods can be a strategic choice. You might, for instance, use spreadsheets for data collection and visualization tools to communicate findings effectively.

As a final point, the choice between low-tech and high-tech strategies should harmonize with your organization's capacities, goals, and available resources. Commencing with low-tech methodologies can establish a solid groundwork, with the potential to incorporate high-tech approaches as your data analysis expertise and resources grow. Adopting a hybrid approach provides the adaptability to harness the advantages of both methods, enabling collective decision-making driven by open data for the greater social good.

NOTES

1   Wakely, E., & Carson, J. (2011). Historical recovery heroes – Florence Nightingale. *Mental Health and Social Inclusion*, 15(1), 24–28.
2   Pfettscher, S. A. (2021). Florence Nightingale: Modern nursing. *Nursing Theorists and Their Work E-Book*, 52.
3   Andrews, R. (2022). How Florence Nightingale changed data visualization forever. *Scientific American*, 327(2), 78–85.
4   Population Reference Bureau. (n.d.). Milestones and Moments in Global Census History. https://www.prb.org/resources/milestones-and-moments-in-global-census-history/#:~:text=3800%20BCE%20The%20Babylonian%20Empire,living%20in%2012.4%20million%20households
5   Zhang, W. (2008). The Yellow Register Archives of Imperial Ming China. *Libraries & the Cultural Record*, 43, 148–175.
6   Steiner, S., & Becker, C. M. (2019). How marriages based on bride capture differ. *Demographic Research*, 41, 579–592.

War of the Words

Unearthing Misinformation

14

On October 30, 1938, police station phone lines across the United States of America were ringing off the hook. Aliens existed, and the Martians were coming to invade.

Instances of hysteria erupted on the streets, with traffic jams forming as people tried to leave their cities for the safety of the countryside, seeking shelter.

All this panic was due to people finishing their evening meals and retiring to their sitting rooms to settle down in front of the radio to listen to one of the leading radio stations in the country, WABC, shortly after 8 p.m.

"Ladies and gentlemen, we interrupt our program of dance music to bring you a special bulletin from the Intercontinental Radio News. At 20 minutes before 8, central time, Professor Farrell of the Mount Jennings Observatory, Chicago, Illinois, reports observing several explosions of incandescent gas, occurring at regular intervals on the planet Mars."

What they were listening to was, of course, fiction: "War of the Worlds" by Orson Welles. If they were sitting in front of the radio at 8 p.m. sharp, they would not have missed the disclaimers at the beginning, stating it was a dramatization.

The aftermath of the War of the Worlds incident provides a compelling showcase of the repercussions stemming from the consumption of misinformation (Figure 14.1).

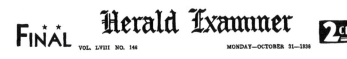

FINAL — **Herald Examiner** — VOL. LVIII NO. 146 — MONDAY—OCTOBER 31—1938 — **2 CENTS**

RADIO FAKE SCARES NATION

FIGURE 14.1 A redrawn cover of the front page of the Chicago Herald and Examiner from the following day in 1938.

DOI: 10.1201/9781032724645-14

The Orson Welles radio broadcast of H.G. Wells' "War of the Worlds" in 1938 is frequently cited as one of the earliest and most renowned instances of mass hysteria triggered by misinformation in modern media. Although not the inaugural case of misinformation, it distinguishes itself through the profound impact it had and the widespread panic it stirred among listeners who genuinely regarded the fictional broadcast as a legitimate news report. This incident underscored the formidable influence of the media, notably radio, in shaping public perception and behavior, particularly during moments of crisis.

This incident shows the real power of storytelling and media in shaping public perception. It highlighted the importance of recognizing that information can spread rapidly and easily, with untold impact. While Wells himself may not have intended to spread misinformation, the events surrounding the broadcast emphasize the need for responsible communication to avoid unintended consequences.

Misinformation has emerged as a potent force, capable of exerting a profound influence on our lives. Misinformation, simply put, is information that is false, deceptive, or misleading in nature. It's the kind of data that lacks a foundation in facts, evidence, or reality, yet it manages to permeate the fabric of our daily existence.

It can manifest in numerous guises, from the whispers of rumors to the bold headlines of fabricated news articles, and from the viral spread of inaccuracies on social media platforms to the distortion of data that underpins critical decisions. In this age of rapid information dissemination, the importance of verifying information from trusted sources cannot be overstated.

The spread of it is more than just an innocuous nuisance; it's a force that can reshape our beliefs, guide our choices, jeopardize our well-being, strain our social bonds, sway policy decisions, and even undermine the foundations of trust in our institutions. Whether it's the realm of politics, health, or our daily interactions, the consequences of misinformation ripple through our lives, demanding our vigilance and critical thinking in navigating the complex landscape of information.

These days, misinformation has become an integral part of our daily lives. I'm sure if you are thumbing through social media on your phone, you will find misinformation, from something as innocent as somebody recording a video pretending they are in a different place to make the recording more interesting to more sinister stuff such as phishing scams. However, valuable lessons can be gleaned from this ongoing challenge.

In regards to protecting our communities, we can harness the power of data as a valuable ally in our fight against misinformation.

Firstly, it's essential to empower community members to become vigilant fact-checkers. Encourage them to diligently cross-reference news and claims with reputable data sources, thereby ensuring the accuracy of the information they are consuming. By organizing informative workshops and webinars, you can equip residents with effective data verification skills, enabling them to confidently distinguish between facts and misinformation.

Additionally, leverage the potency of data visualization to simplify complex information, transforming it into easily digestible visuals. These compelling graphics serve as invaluable assets for presenting accurate information, effectively countering the deceptive visual elements or graphs often tied to false narratives. By providing visually compelling evidence, communities can effectively debunk misinformation and promote data-backed insights, but keep it simple.

Advocacy for transparency in data collection and reporting is also crucial, not only within your community but also from external sources. Collaborate with local government agencies and organizations to champion open data policies and initiatives that encourage data sharing. By fostering a culture of transparency, you empower your community to access reliable information and discern the truth from falsehoods effectively.

You can also try to implement data literacy initiatives within your community, with a particular focus on equipping residents, especially students who are highly exposed to misinformation, with essential skills to critically assess information and discern misinformation. Promoting data literacy empowers individuals to navigate the digital landscape effectively, making them less susceptible to misinformation and better prepared to contribute to fact-based discussions.

To enhance the impact of your efforts, raise awareness about the pivotal role open data plays in combating misinformation. Engage with community members through local events, social media campaigns, and informative sessions to illustrate how open data can be a cornerstone of accurate information dissemination. By highlighting its significance, you encourage individuals to value open data as a tool for truth and authenticity in the information age. Encourage community participation in fact-checking efforts by analyzing open data. Together, these are strategies that empower communities to stand strong against the tide of misinformation and ensure the dissemination of accurate, reliable information (Figure 14.2).

We can't talk about misinformation without addressing its impact on vaccines and the context of COVID-19. Nigeria has a historical struggle with vaccine-related misinformation, and this issue resurfaced during the coronavirus pandemic.

In the past, Nigeria has faced a significant challenge related to vaccine hesitancy and refusal. This issue has been fueled by false rumors and a decline in public trust. For instance, in 2003,[1] there was a baseless rumor that the oral polio vaccine contained certain undesirable substances, such as porcine material and sterilizing agents. This misinformation prompted a large-scale boycott of polio vaccination in northern Nigeria. The outcomes were grave, causing a resurgence of polio instances and the reintroduction of wild polio in 20 countries across Africa and Asia.

This setback not only impeded polio eradication efforts in Nigeria but also had far-reaching implications for the wider African region.

In 2017, a deeply harmful rumor spread like wildfire across Nigeria, alleging that the country's military was forcefully administering the monkeypox vaccine to children.[2] This alarming misinformation campaign resulted in an immediate and unsettling response from parents, who swiftly withdrew their children from school. Even more concerning was the enduring impact of this false narrative on future vaccine acceptance rates within the affected communities, serving as a stark reminder of the far-reaching consequences of misinformation on public health initiatives and community well-being.

In Delta State, the fight against COVID-19 has been accompanied by a surge in misinformation and a breeding ground for the Nigerian infodemic. The University of Benin,[3] surveying 2,500 respondents, revealed a stark reality: only 27.68% were willing to receive the COVID-19 vaccine. What's driving this hesitancy? Widespread misinformation, particularly on social media, is a major factor. Alarmingly, 52% of those with social media access admit they don't verify health information with medical experts.

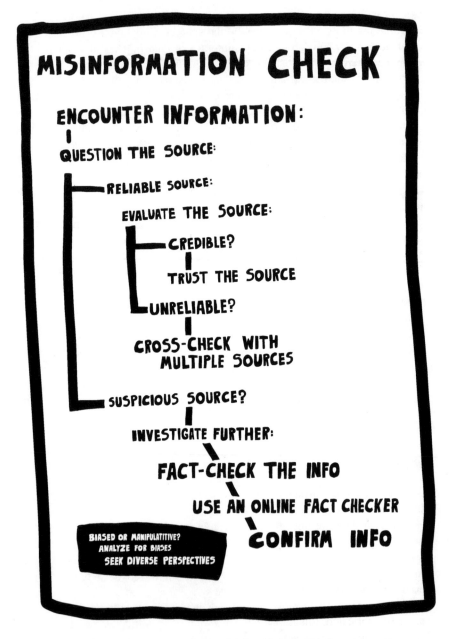

FIGURE 14.2   What paths can you take to check misinformation?

Prominent figures, including the traditional ruler Ooni of Ife and former Chairman of Nigeria's Independent Electoral Commission Maurice Iwu,[4] also promoted herbal alternatives to fortify against COVID-19. Ben Amodu, a doctor, claimed his herbs could prevent the virus. The Federal Government of Nigeria even considered meeting with practitioners of traditional herbal medicine due to the proliferation of local concoctions against COVID-19.

The spread of misinformation is harmful in various ways, not just in influencing how we think but in its potential to genuinely cost lives. Unfortunately, the COVID-19 pandemic provided fertile ground for getting poor fact checks or downright sinister information out there.

In Qom City, Iran, for instance, the consequences were devastating. More than 700[5] people lost their lives after ingesting toxic methanol in the thought process that it was a cure for the virus. This surge in cases, some resulting in blindness and severe organ damage, occurred in the early course of the pandemic. Iran has been grappling with one of the most severe outbreaks of COVID-19 in the Middle East, with thousands of deaths and confirmed cases. Tragically, some individuals, desperate for a cure, resorted to consuming methanol, unaware of its deadly consequences.

Even though the source of the misinformation was unclear, the British newspaper *The Telegraph* stated that "there have been reports that newspaper stories wrongly suggesting a British school teacher and others had cured themselves by drinking whisky had been widely shared in Iran[6]" was the culprit.

Transitioning from the discussion of COVID-19 to the HIV problem in Africa, it's essential to highlight an alarming episode during Yahya Jammeh's presidency in the Gambia from 1994 to 2017. During this period, Jammeh made highly dubious claims about his ability to cure HIV/AIDS[7] using unconventional herbal treatments combined with spiritual rituals. Oh, and you could only use the cure on specific days of the week; otherwise, it wouldn't work. Let's not forget that.

The fallout from this in the community was massive, as it convinced people living with HIV/AIDS to stop treatments, including antiretroviral drugs, which are medically recognized for managing the virus.

The ramifications of Jammeh's misinformation sowed doubt and false hope among HIV/AIDS sufferers across Africa, contributing to the virus's further spread. Health authorities and global organizations unequivocally criticized his statements for their potential to inflict harm and hinder public health endeavors.

Following the election of the then-new President Adama Barrow, the Gambia established the Truth, Reconciliation, and Reparations Commission (TRRC) to investigate human rights violations during Jammeh's time in office.

Setting up truth commissions is not a novel approach to addressing violations in Africa, but even they are not safe from misinformation. In Sierra Leone, for example, mistrust in the process was circulated, including widespread rumors claiming that there was a secret tunnel[8] between the Special Court for Sierra Leone and the Truth Commission.

In all of these scenarios, social media, particularly WhatsApp,[9] played a significant role in spreading misinformation during the pandemic. False information, whether intentionally fabricated (disinformation) or shared unknowingly (misinformation), found an easy avenue for transmission.

Returning to Nigeria, the spread of misinformation remains a challenge to this day and poses a real threat to their democracy.[10]

But since NGOs in the country have taken up a prominent role in the ongoing fight against misinformation, you could argue that they are doing a better job than their government, particularly in a country where false narratives and "fake news" have been a pervasive issue. They are taking the fight against misinformation, putting importance on what it poses to society, and are actively engaged in various initiatives to combat it. They conduct fact-checking campaigns, organize training and workshops to enhance media literacy, and collaborate with local communities to disseminate accurate information. Moreover, they work in partnership with government agencies and healthcare institutions to promote reliable information and counter the spread of false narratives, contributing significantly to the fight against misinformation in Nigeria's information landscape.

Misinformation and elections go hand in hand; they can impact public perception and even threaten the integrity of the voting process. There are many NGOs that are dedicated to upholding democratic values and human rights in Africa, and they actively work to address the issue of fake news that affects Nigerians on a daily basis. The rise of artificial intelligence tools for spreading misinformation[11] further complicates the situation, making the role of these organizations in debunking false narratives even more critical. By equipping journalists and the public with the necessary tools and knowledge to identify and combat misinformation, these NGOs are playing a vital role in preserving the integrity of information in Nigeria.

What can you do? A good start is to consider launching an awareness campaign in your local area, a strategy that benefits not only your organization but also has a far-reaching impact on the broader community. Beyond the organizational perspective, this initiative serves as a great public relations opportunity, underscoring your dedication to knowledge sharing and community betterment.

Let's show you how to do it. You can use this as a foundation to make your own:

CAMPAIGN PLAN: EQUIPPING OUR COMMUNITY WITH FACT-CHECKING SKILLS

Campaign Objective: Empower community members with essential fact-checking skills to effectively combat misinformation.

CAMPAIGN PHASES AND ACTIVITIES

Phase 1: Campaign Initiation

1. Assemble a dedicated campaign team, including community volunteers, educators, and local influencers passionate about promoting fact-checking skills.
2. Develop a captivating campaign name, slogan, and logo to establish a memorable brand identity.
3. Establish an exclusive campaign website and social media profiles to facilitate outreach and information dissemination.
4. Forge partnerships with local government entities, businesses, and community organizations to introduce fact-checking programs.

Phase 2: Building Awareness

1. Launch an engaging social media campaign featuring informative posts, videos, and eye-catching infographics to emphasize the significance of fact-checking.

2. Organize local awareness events such as seminars, workshops, and panel discussions, with guest appearances by experts and educators.
3. Distribute campaign promotional materials such as flyers and posters throughout the community to broaden visibility.
4. Enlist local influencers to endorse the campaign and share practical fact-checking tips on their platforms.

Phase 3: Educational Workshops

1. Host a series of fact-checking workshops catering to various age groups within the community.
2. Collaborate with local government agencies, businesses, and community groups to incorporate fact-checking modules into their existing programs.
3. Offer online webinars and interactive sessions to accommodate those unable to attend in person.
4. Provide participants with comprehensive fact-checking toolkits and an array of resources for future reference.
5. Make sure you collect data from the activities; this could make a great open dataset.

Phase 4: Fact-Checking Challenge

1. Initiate a community-wide fact-checking challenge, motivating participants to verify information using reliable open data sources.
2. Create a dedicated online platform where participants can submit their findings and compete for recognition.
3. Recognize and reward the most proficient and accurate fact-checkers with prizes, certificates, or other incentives.
4. Showcase successful fact-checkers in campaign success stories and through local media.

Phase 5: Continuous Engagement

1. Sustain a consistent online presence with regular updates on fact-checking guidelines, tips, and relevant news articles.
2. Collaborate with local authorities, businesses, and community organizations to conduct periodic fact-checking assessments, tracking progress and improvements.
3. Foster community involvement through routine Q&A sessions and interactive discussions on fact-checking-related topics.
4. Leverage community feedback to refine and expand the campaign's educational offerings, ensuring they remain responsive to evolving needs.

Phase 6: Evaluation and Impact Assessment

1. Conduct surveys and assessments to measure the campaign's influence on community members' fact-checking capabilities.

2. Share campaign achievements and success stories through local media outlets, celebrating the positive impact on the community.
3. Compile a comprehensive campaign report detailing key milestones achieved and valuable lessons learned throughout the process.
4. Conclude the campaign with a celebratory event, acknowledging exceptional participants and dedicated supporters.

Key Message: "Empower yourself with fact-checking skills. Be a responsible consumer of information and a guardian against misinformation."

Remember: Encourage community participation in fact-checking efforts through the analysis of open data. Crowdsourcing can serve as a valuable resource for identifying and debunking false information circulating within your community. These strategies, when employed together, empower communities to stand resolute against the rising tide of misinformation, ensuring the dissemination of accurate, reliable information.

CAMPAIGN EVALUATION METRICS

1. Number of participants in workshops and webinars.
2. Increase in fact-checking assessment scores among students and community members.
3. Participation and engagement metrics on campaign social media platforms.
4. A number of fact-checking challenge submissions.
5. Community feedback and testimonials.
6. Extent of media coverage and reach.
7. Growth in the campaign's online and offline communities.

By actively engaging local government bodies, businesses, and community organizations in fact-checking initiatives, you can foster a collaborative approach that amplifies the campaign's impact and encourages the widespread adoption of fact-checking skills across the community.

Near the end of 2023, following the Hamas attack on Israel, Elon Musk found himself in hot water with the EU over alleged disinformation, including the use of "repurposed old images"[12] shared on his X platform. This caution coincided with the enforcement of the Digital Services Act (DSA),[13] which governs content on social media platforms. Non-compliance with these regulations may lead to severe consequences, including significant fines, or even the possibility of X being completely blocked within the EU.

To the European Union, the DSA represents a step forward in updating their legal framework for digital life, focusing on key aspects such as tackling illegal content, ensuring honest advertising, and combating disinformation. It's important to note that while the DSA includes a voluntary code of practice intended as guidance for companies, not all platforms have chosen to participate. For instance, X decided not to join this voluntary initiative, in contrast to their social media counterparts such as Facebook, Google, and TikTok. However, regardless of participation, all digital platforms must adhere to the DSA's rules, which empower the EU to apply strict fines for non-compliance.

On the same subject, via X, several instances involving misinformation and false content have come to light.[14] Among them are misleading videos, including a viral clip that inaccurately portrayed a Hamas fighter downing an Israeli helicopter, which was actually sourced from the video game Arma 3. Another video displayed an attack on an Israeli woman, but upon investigation, it was revealed to have been filmed in Guatemala back in 2015. These cases highlight the challenge of discerning accurate information in the digital age.

Thierry Breton, the EU commissioner responsible for overseeing the DSA, expressed his concerns to Musk in a strongly worded letter, urging prompt action to address this critical issue. Breton underlined that the DSA imposes precise obligations concerning content moderation, emphasizing that Musk had previously opted out of the voluntary code of practice established by the EU. In contrast, major players such as Facebook, Google, and TikTok actively participated in this code, taking measures to combat disinformation as specified by the regulations.

In the aftermath of the 2011 Arab Spring revolutions, a new kind of war unfolded[15]— one fought not on traditional battlefields but on the digital frontiers of social media. What had initially begun as a wave of pro-democracy movements, facilitated by platforms such as Facebook and Twitter, soon evolved into a complex and contentious online landscape. Social media became the arena where various forces clashed, with consequences that rippled across the globe.

One of the most striking outcomes of this digital conflict was the emergence of extremist groups, notably ISIS (Islamic State of Iraq and Syria). With a remarkable grasp of social media, ISIS harnessed these platforms to disseminate its radical ideology, recruit fighters from diverse corners of the world, and shock the world with gruesome videos and images of violence. Social media served as the global stage where the group showcased its brutality and drew in recruits.

The Syrian conflict became a focal point of this digital propaganda war. Supporters of different factions, opposition groups, and foreign actors engaged in a relentless battle of narratives. Misinformation flowed freely, blurring the lines between fact and fiction and manipulating public perceptions through cleverly crafted social media campaigns. In this digital battleground, discerning the truth became a formidable challenge.

Misinformation gives credence to powerful people from a shadowy perspective to attempt to erase history and change the narrative. No one understands this more than the people of Syria, even years after their break for freedom from the Bashar al-Assad regime.

Michael Brenner, of Data4Change, an organization that defends human rights with data, knows all about how online misinformation has far-reaching consequences. He has first-hand experience working with dedicated doctors, compassionate humanitarians, and staunch human rights defenders in Syria, many of whom found themselves contending with real-life fallout due to the pervasive spread of disinformation.

Witnessing the profound toll exacted on society by the proliferation of false narratives in our closely connected global landscape, individuals just like him are leveraging their digital skills to address this pressing issue.

"In our current digital age, navigating misinformation has become a real challenge. However, with activism, we can uphold the truth and accuracy. It's not about how tech-savvy you are; if you're sharing and consuming information, then there's a responsibility to ensure it's accurate and truthful. By working together, staying educated, and drawing from our collective knowledge, we can halt the tide of disinformation. Authenticity and radically clear communication are key. There's no external savior; the responsibility to foster an informed tomorrow lies with us."

Collectively, we require innovative solutions, and the most impactful ideas often originate from human rights defenders who are in dire need of support. To achieve this, we must engage and mobilize digital activists, some of whom may not even recognize themselves as activists. The fight against misinformation necessitates a collaborative effort that combines the strengths of both physical and digital activism.

NOTES

1 Wonodi, C., Obi-Jeff, C., Adewumi, F., Keluo-Udeke, S. C., Gur-Arie, R., Krubiner, C., ..., & Faden, R. (2022). Conspiracy theories and misinformation about COVID-19 in Nigeria: Implications for vaccine demand generation communications. *Vaccine*, 40(13), 2114–2121.

2 Nnaemeka, F. O., & Onunkwor, S. I. (2021). Believability of social media posts: A study of alleged forceful injection of monkey pox virus in school children. *Nnamdi Azikiwe University Journal of Communication and Media Studies*, 2, 1–23. https://doi.org/10.47851/naujocommed.v2i1.121

3 Kingsley, E. N., & Chukwuemeke, I. J. (2022). Investigating the effect of Infodemic on the Perception and Willingness to take the COVID–19 vaccine in delta state, Nigeria. *Journal of Community Health Research*, 11(3): 191–201.

4 Alo, O. (2020, May 7). Coronavirus Treatment: Ooni of Ife, Researchers Like Professor Maurice Iwu Dey among Nigerians Wey Claim to Get 'Otumokpo' Traditional Herbs to Cure Covid-19 Disease. *BBC Pidgin*. https://www.bbc.com/pidgin/tori-52578762.

5 Aghababaeian, H., Hamdanieh, L., & Ostadtaghizadeh, A. (2020). Alcohol intake in an attempt to fight COVID-19: A medical myth in Iran. *Alcohol*, 88, 29–32.

6 Farmer, B. (2020, April 28). Toxic Alcohol Kills More Than 700 in Iran Following False Reports It Wards Off Coronavirus. *The Telegraph*. https://www.telegraph.co.uk/global-health/science-and-disease/toxic-alcohol-kills-700-iran-following-false-reports-ward-coronavirus/

7 Bosha, S. L., Adeniyi, M., Ivan, J., Ghiaseddin, R., Minteh, F., Barrow, L. F., & Kuye, R. (2019). The impact of the presidential alternative treatment program on people living with HIV and the Gambian HIV response. *Health and Human Rights*, 21(1), 239.

8 van den Berg, S. (2022). Between hope and expectation: Understanding ordinary ex-combatant agency in Sierra Leone's TRC. *Conflict, Security & Development*, 22(2), 119–141.

9 Romm, T. (2020, March 2). Fake Cures and Other Coronavirus Conspiracy Theories Are Flooding WhatsApp, Leaving Governments and Users with a 'Sense of Panic.' *The Washington Post*. https://www.washingtonpost.com/technology/2020/03/02/whatsapp-coronavirus-misinformation/

10 Mefo Takambou, M. (2023, July 20). Nigeria Takes Steps to Tackle 'Rampant' Disinformation. *DW News*. https://www.dw.com/en/nigeria-takes-steps-to-tackle-rampant-disinformation/a-66297788

11 Fried, I. (2023, July 10). How AI Will Turbocharge Misinformation — And What We Can Do about It. *Axios AI+*. https://www.axios.com/2023/07/10/ai-misinformation-response-measures

12 O'Carroll, L. (2023, October 10). EU Warns Elon Musk over 'Disinformation' on X about Hamas Attack. *The Guardian*. https://www.theguardian.com/technology/2023/oct/10/eu-warns-elon-musk-over-disinformation-about-hamas-attack-on-x

13 European Commission. (n.d.). The Digital Services Act Package. https://digital-strategy.ec.europa.eu/en/policies/digital-services-act-package

14 Bond, S. (2023, October 10). Video Game Clips and Old Videos Are Flooding Social Media about Israel and Gaza. *NPR*. https://www.npr.org/2023/10/10/1204755129/video-game-clips-and-old-videos-are-flooding-social-media-about-israel-and-gaza

15 Shehabat, A. (2012). The social media cyber-war: The unfolding events in the Syrian revolution 2011. *Global Media Journal: Australian Edition*, 6(2).

Influencing Change with Data, North Macedonia as a Case Study

15

Skopje, the quirky capital of North Macedonia, is renowned as "the city of statues." In this eccentric city, a fusion of ancient heritage and contemporary glamour meets amid a backdrop of political controversies intertwined with an astonishing array of monuments.

Skopje's transformation is both captivating and puzzling, creating a truly unique destination.

There is a joke that the locals say that there are more statues than people, and one of their favorite pastimes is seeing how many statues they can count in an hour. Don't worry, there are plenty.

So, picture yourself strolling through Skopje, doing as the locals do, surrounded by these statues at every turn. It's as if the city has come alive to pay homage to legendary Macedonian figures from the past. But there is something that is somewhat unsettling: these statues are not relics of bygone eras. They are sparkling, brand-new creations that adorn the cityscape, reminiscent of glitzy ornaments in a Las Vegas hotel.

However, behind the grandeur lies a tale of political turmoil and public discontent. So much so that former prime minister Nikola Gruevski[1] cannot even return home without fear of arrest, which speaks volumes about what we would perceive to be the lingering consequences. Yet, the controversies surrounding Skopje's statues go beyond politics; they symbolize a clash of visions, attracting both tourists and disdain in equal measure.

You may be wondering about the cost of having a statue at every corner. Brace yourself—over 600 million pounds and counting![2] But it's not just the staggering price tag that has raised eyebrows; it's the underlying corruption and cronyism that have come to light. One construction firm, DG Beton AD, has received a staggering 216 million euros,[3] leaving citizens questioning the government's priorities. The original budget for the city revamp was 80 million euros, which is a massive number in itself, considering one in six people in North Macedonia live below the poverty line according to World Bank Data.[4]

DOI: 10.1201/9781032724645-15

Skopje's statue spree was not just about aesthetics—it was a calculated political maneuver. The ambitious Skopje 2014 redevelopment program aimed to revive the ancient heritage of the Ancient Macedonians,[5] sparking heated debates. On one hand, there was a nationalist push to reclaim the region's historical roots and establish a connection to the ancient Kingdom of Macedon. On the other hand, Greece vehemently protested,[6] accusing North Macedonia of appropriating Greek historical figures such as Alexander the Great.

Amidst the chaos and discord, there is a glimmer of hope—Skopje 2014 Uncovered,[7] an exceptional open data project initiated by the Balkan Investigative Journalist Network. This project lays bare the costs and builders of each statue, exposing the corruption and criminality that plagued Skopje's governance. Data storytelling emerges as a powerful tool, empowering citizens and holding those in power accountable.

The aftermath of Skopje 2014 sparked what was called the "colorful revolution," where thousands of people took to the streets in protest of the revelations, pelting statues with paint bombs and filling them with foundations of soap bubbles in protest against the then government.

North Macedonia stands as a compelling case study, illustrating the significant impact of data storytelling in driving civic transformation despite a government's hesitation to embrace transparency. The untapped potential of this platform sparks thoughts of a future where Skopje's data-driven revolution paves the way for a vibrant digital social culture recognized worldwide. Although the destination remains a work in progress, the journey has already commenced. For those keen to harness the power of data for impactful campaigns, Skopje's narrative offers a valuable source of inspiration (Figure 15.1).

Its journey has had an immense impact on how data can have a hand in revealing truths, igniting civic transformation, and advocating for transparency from those in authority. It has taught us lessons about the transformative force of information, the significance of civic involvement, and the unwavering determination of a community aspiring for a more promising tomorrow.

The Balkan Investigative Reporting Network, commonly referred to as BIRN, operates as a consortium of non-governmental organizations dedicated to championing fundamental values such as freedom of speech, human rights, and democracy in Southern and Eastern Europe. The core mission of BIRN is to empower individuals to exercise their rights by providing accurate and pertinent information while fostering opportunities for civic engagement in democratic processes.

BIRN's decision to embark on this extensive investigation was motivated by a commitment to transparency and accountability in public projects. At the heart of their mission was a drive to shed light on how taxpayer money was being allocated and spent. The team at BIRN recognized the importance of open data and access to public information as fundamental tools for an informed citizenry. By leveraging data obtained through the Law on Free Access to Public Information,[8] public procurement records, and official government reports, BIRN unveiled a web of contracts, agreements, and discrepancies that had remained concealed for years.

As I mentioned, the heart of this financial saga led to the construction company "Beton," which emerged as the project's chief beneficiary, securing a staggering one-third of the total funds allocated. BIRN's investigation didn't stop at construction contracts;

FIGURE 15.1   Thousands of people fill Macedonia Square, Skopje, as part of the Colorful Revolution.

Photo Credit: Robert Atanasovski.

it ventured into the often-opaque world of author fees. Notably, sculptor Valentina Stevanovska took center stage, her work encompassing iconic monuments and sculptures dotting Skopje's landscape and collectively garnering nearly 3 million euros.

To tackle comparable challenges and exert pressure on local governments to release more open data, gaining insight into initiatives like Skopje 2014 Uncovered becomes essential. While it may not directly match the gravity of the issue at hand most of the time, valuable lessons can be drawn from their impact and influence.

"We spent a month, going from a monument to a monument, from a building to a building. We took pictures of each one of them and pinned them on a map. Made folders for each one of them and that's how we started the process of gathering information, with no clue of what we'll find out at the end. That's the most boring thing, working and thinking, why I am doing this, what if it's for nothing, what if we don't find a thing?"

Said Meri Jordanovska, an editor, data journalist, Skopje resident, and digital activist who was heavily involved in designing Skopje 2014 Uncovered, who actually calls the project her "baby," shared insights on how they built the project.

"We sent requests for Free access to public information, according to Law, to each institution involved in Skopje 2014—we requested for every agreement between them and the construction companies/authors for every object of Skopje 2014, including the annexes of the agreements. That took months—to ask the right questions, so the institutions couldn't fool you. Also, the thing was that the agreements were on low amounts—for example, 4 million euros. But the annexes on that agreement were huge, sometimes 10 times larger than the amount in the initial agreement between the construction company/author and the institution. There was one building, for example, with a total of 80 annexes on the initial agreement. So we gathered these documents and put each amount and the number of the agreement in Excel tables."

But there were valuable lessons that were learned.

"The second stage was checking the Public Procurement Bureau, where all the agreements between public institutions and private investors are published. It was hard to dig into that public database because it was quite confusing, but we managed to download all the documents needed. It's a strange thing—after we published Skopje 2014 Uncovered, all these documents suddenly 'disappeared' from the website of the Public Procurement Bureau, so there was a lesson—download and print screen before you publish!"

Meri and the technical team who designed the project knew the importance of making the data clear and understandable to achieve maximum impact, and the work paid off.

"Once we were done, we could finally see the findings and that was the big moment—we had a very clear picture of what was going on" going on to highlight the need to make it as concise as possible "to make the database as searchable as possible—by authors, by construction companies, by objects, by amounts, by institutions. It was very important to make it as user-friendly as possible, to make sure that when the audience clicks on anything, they will get a result, comparisons, and an explanation."

"Always, when making a database, we should keep in mind one thing—we are making something that will stay forever—for further investigations, as a tool, for further publications and we should make it as close to people as possible and as searchable as possible."

In 2022, I was in the city myself as I was working at the International Open Data Conference, hosted by USAID, where I organized a policy hackathon called 'Roadmap to Open Data.' This event focused on procedures and policies, the creation of a national open data portal, and the development of essential technical skills. The goal was to guide institutions and non-governmental organizations in incorporating an open data culture, emphasizing transparency and collaboration between governments and NGOs in North Macedonia.

Being there and having the opportunity to train people from the country was truly insightful. Participants shared their concerns about North Macedonia nearly sleepwalking into an authoritarian dictatorship and expressed their worries about living in the country at that time. Their emphasis on transparency and the value they place on it really hit home for me, highlighting how important open data has been in shaping a path to democracy in the country.

I also learned about the value of government jobs in the country and how they struggle to attract talent due to how poorly they pay. This is really interesting because in Western Europe, government roles are seen as good, well-paid jobs, and governments are able to attract a wide array of talent who can bring new ideas and thinking and revolutionize services. North Macedonia, however, cannot, which is an important consideration in the aspect of using open data as an international development resource; a one-size approach doesn't fit all.

With that in mind, to tackle comparable challenges and exert pressure on local governments to release more open data, gaining insight into initiatives like Skopje 2014 Uncovered becomes essential. To put it bluntly, North Macedonia's relationship with open data is purely from the ground up. It is a collective project that was born out of sheer passion and conviction to learn from its past and to make sure it never happens again.

Drawing from my experiences, here are key steps to consider if we were to implement them ourselves:

1. **Recognize the Importance of Open Data:** Open data offers numerous opportunities for individuals, businesses, and communities. It enables evidence-based decision-making, fosters accountability, and encourages public participation. By emphasizing these benefits, we can raise awareness about the significance of open data and its impact on civic life.

2. **Assess the Current Situation:** Before taking action, it's essential to evaluate the status of open data in your local government. Research existing policies, initiatives, and available datasets, if any. Identify gaps and areas where data is lacking or inaccessible. This assessment will provide a clear understanding of the challenges ahead.

3. **Build a Coalition:** Creating a coalition of like-minded individuals, organizations, and activists is crucial to amplifying your voice and advocating for open data. Collaborate with local tech communities, nonprofits, journalists, and other stakeholders who share your vision. Pool resources, expertise, and influence to tackle the issue more effectively.

4. **Engage with Local Government:** Initiate a constructive dialogue with your local government representatives to discuss the importance of open data. Present a compelling case, showcasing real-life examples of how open data

initiatives have benefited other communities. Demonstrate how open data can foster economic growth, improve service delivery, and enhance transparency in governance. Request a commitment from the government to prioritize and expand their open data efforts.

5. **Raise Public Awareness:** Educating the public about the value of open data is crucial for generating support and building momentum. Utilize social media, local events, and public forums to raise awareness about the benefits of open data and the limitations faced by your community. Share success stories from other cities or countries where open data has made a significant impact. Encourage citizens to demand access to data and voice their concerns to local representatives.

6. **Empower Data Journalism:** Support and collaborate with journalists who can investigate and report on the lack of open data in your local government. Journalistic investigations can help uncover potential corruption or inefficiencies associated with data access. Publish articles, opinion pieces, and investigative reports that shed light on the issue and capture public attention.

7. **Develop Alternative Data Sources:** If your local government is unwilling to release open data, consider creating alternative data sources through citizen-led initiatives. Skopje 2014 Uncovered serves as an inspiring example of how citizens can gather and analyze data independently to expose issues and drive change. Establish citizen-led data projects that collect and analyze relevant information, highlighting gaps in official datasets and demonstrating the demand for open data.

8. **Advocate for Policy Change:** Engage with policymakers and legislators to advocate for policy changes that prioritize open data. Lobby for the implementation of open data legislation, transparency regulations, and data-sharing protocols from within.

9. **Monitor Progress and Hold Government Accountable:** Continuously monitor the progress made by your local government in releasing open data. Hold them accountable for their commitments and demand transparency in their actions. Highlight the achievements and positive impacts resulting from open data initiatives. If progress stalls or commitments are not met, mobilize your coalition and the wider public to maintain pressure and advocate for change.

By understanding the journey of digital activists in North Macedonia, we can draw lessons on how to address challenges we may not traditionally consider. Sometimes the obvious approach, which is usually top-down and initiated by data providers, is not always the best, and sometimes we need not be afraid to take measures in our own hands (Figure 15.2).

But as we come to the end of this chapter, what is the legacy of Skopje 2014 Uncovered?

"The reactions from the public were huge. We are living in a country with low standards, lack of hospital equipment, huge poverty and it was a big shock to know that the officials are spending such big amounts that won't bring a better life for the citizens."

This sparked the project being propelled into media outlets across the country and, of course, into the eyes of the law, Jordanovska went on to tell me.

FIGURE 15.2 "Protests against dysfunctional institutions found expression in symbolic paint throwing at 'Skopje 2014'; objects, marking the start of the Colorful Revolution," protest participant Ljuben Dimanovski told me while sharing photos of those events.
Photo Credit: Tomislav Georgiev

"After publishing the database, we had absolutely not one denial from the officials. Actually, we had no reaction at all. It was like nothing happened. But that's what officials do when they want to put something under the carpet. On the other hand, in every publication, and in every investigation, our database (Skopje 2014 Uncovered) was quoted, because it was the only existential thing about the controversial project. We were the only ones who had the documents and the amounts, something that was hidden from the public for a long time and we got many journalism awards for that.

Relying on these documents and our findings, the Special Public Prosecution opened an investigation that lasted for years. We were also called as witnesses because the database was the only 'live' thing related to Skopje 2014 that was based on documents. The initial findings from the prosecution announced in 2023 are that there was money laundering and misuse of the official positions of 15 people, JUST for 11 monuments. The initial findings were that they made agreements with foundries in Italy for huge amounts, but the monuments afterward were made for amounts much lower than that. So the rest of the public money, through offshore companies, this time laundered, was brought back in N. Macedonia through new-formed companies."

However, 10 years on, there was a twist.

"The Government made changes in the Criminal Law, with no public debate, no involvement of the NGOs, and out of the public eye—that every investigation or a court decision in the first degree for an act made before 2013 should be dismissed for further investigation. So that's how nobody took responsibility for the findings and suspicions of crime with the Skopje 2014 project. Only the monuments and the buildings are there to witness and remind us of the controversial and criminal acts of the officials."

Even though those who were responsible may never be brought to justice, one thing is for certain: the project changed the landscape of anti-corruption in the Balkan nation forever, and thanks to the efforts of people like Meri and her colleagues, future decision-makers think twice with the knowing that there is a cohort of vehement change-makers who are more than capable of holding their feet to the fire, and there is much we can learn from their work.

The story of Skopje 2014 Uncovered illustrates the power of data and citizen action to drive change. By following these steps, individuals and communities can pressure their local governments to release more open data. Remember, change is possible when citizens come together, demand transparency, and advocate for justice. Embrace the mindset, stand up for your rights, and be a catalyst for positive transformation in your own community.

NOTES

1 Żornaczuk, T. (2018). Political Effects of Hungary Granting Asylum to the Former Prime Minister of Macedonia. PISM Bulletin, 2. PISM Polski Instytut Spraw Międzynarodowych.
2 Reef, P. (2018). Macedonian Monument Culture Beyond 'Skopje 2014'. *Comparative Southeast European Studies.* https://doi.org/10.1515/soeu-2018-0037
3 Panovska, M. Collective Memory of Macedonia through the Studies of Monuments: An Analysis of the Project 'Skopje 2014'.

4 World Bank. (2023, April). Poverty & Equity Brief: North Macedonia. Europe & Central Asia. https://databankfiles.worldbank.org/public/ddpext_download/poverty/987B9C90-C B9F-4D93-AE8C-750588BF00QA/current/Global_POVEQ_MKD.pdf

5 Vangeli, Anastas (2011): Nation-building ancient Macedonian style: The origins and the effects of the so-called antiquization in Macedonia. *Nationalities Papers*, 39 (1), 16.

6 Reef, P. (2018). Macedonian monument culture beyond 'Skopje 2014'. *Comparative Southeast European Studies*, 66(4), 451–480.

7 BIRN. (2015, August 19). BIRN Macedonia Launches "Skopje 2014 Uncovered" Database. *Balkan Investigative Reporting Network*. https://birn.eu.com/news-and-events/ birn-macedonia-launches-skopje-2014-uncovered-database/

8 Open Government Partnership. (2014). Availability of All Public Information on the Web Sites of the Information Holders (All Holders) (MK0058). In Action Plan: Macedonia, Second Action Plan, 2014–2016. Action Plan Cycle: 2014. https://www.opengovpartner-ship.org/members/north-macedonia/commitments/MK0058/

Punk as Hell

16

DIY Digitalism and How Open-Source Makes Releasing Your Data Easy

Even though the waking world is falling apart, technologies are advancing at a scary rate, making our lives both easier and weirder. We've seen people falling in love with AI chatbots[1] and even fitting rats with brain-to-brain[2] interfaces for remote collaboration (thankfully, that idea didn't take off).

To build most of these technological wonders, you need money. And the people who have that money often have a different perspective on its value. While some invest their time and resources into creating toasters that can text your friends or smart belts that tell you that you are getting too fat, others may find this kind of stuff wasteful. But, let's be honest, we all love a bit of absurdity.

In Albania, open source is a lifeline for many technologists. It's a tool for education and capacity building, a bridge to connect with individuals worldwide who have access to essential data. Albanians adapt and customize open-source platforms to suit their unique needs, thanks to the collaborative and open nature of these resources. Open source remains a powerful asset for digital activists (Figure 16.1).

The communist regime in Albania cultivated a culture of deep distrust, leading citizens to view each other with suspicion and eroding societal trust. This tactic aimed to quell dissent by conditioning individuals to be wary of neighbors and acquaintances. Additionally, the regime promoted "extreme friend-foe thinking,[3]" categorizing people as either friends or enemies with little middle ground, stemming from the divisive nature of communist ideology.

Importantly, these attitudes persist in post-communist Albania, influencing how people interact. Despite the regime's demise, its legacy of distrust, which shapes social dynamics and political discourse, emphasizes the lasting impact of these patterns.

Albanians harbor mixed feelings toward digital technology, and it is a massive concern in the context of digitization. Research has suggested that citizens still hesitate to

DOI: 10.1201/9781032724645-16

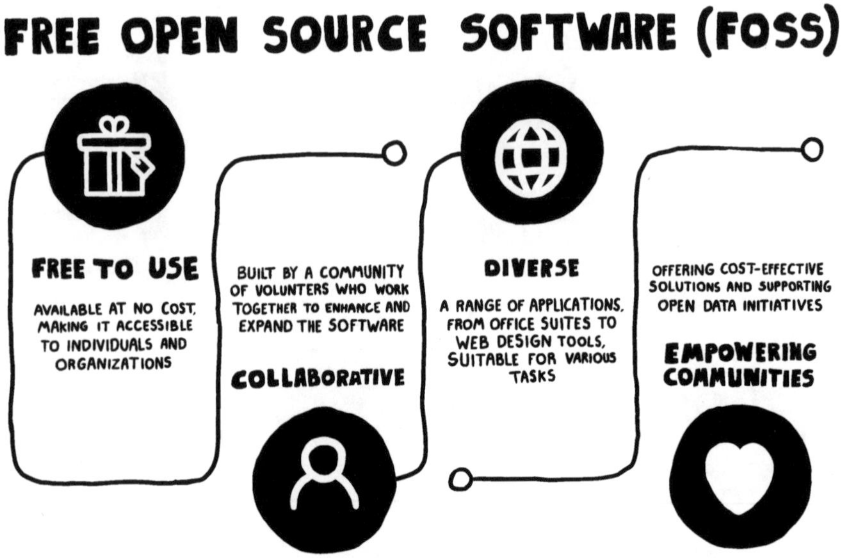

FREE OPEN SOURCE SOFTWARE (FOSS)

FREE TO USE

AVAILABLE AT NO COST, MAKING IT ACCESSIBLE TO INDIVIDUALS AND ORGANIZATIONS

BUILT BY A COMMUNITY OF VOLUNTERS WHO WORK TOGETHER TO ENHANCE AND EXPAND THE SOFTWARE

COLLABORATIVE

DIVERSE

A RANGE OF APPLICATIONS, FROM OFFICE SUITES TO WEB DESIGN TOOLS, SUITABLE FOR VARIOUS TASKS

OFFERING COST-EFFECTIVE SOLUTIONS AND SUPPORTING OPEN DATA INITIATIVES

EMPOWERING COMMUNITIES

FIGURE 16.1 The pillars of free and open source software.

use digital services unless they are confident they are secure; their level of trust and security within digital services is a vital element.[4]

Much like the potential for digital initiatives to originate within a community, Tirana's transformation through DIY initiatives illustrates the profound impact of small actions on radical change. Inheriting a city mired in mismanagement, corruption, and rampant crime[5] back in 2000, Edi Rama, one of Albania's most prominent DIY champions and an artist, took up the mantle of Tirana's mayor. The city was downtrodden, and without the funds for an extensive reconstruction of its forest of brutalist flats, he painted them a wash of stunning colors and patterns, which completely changed the landscape. This act vividly demonstrates how small actions can spark monumental transformations.

Similar to the way you can transform communities by simply rolling up your sleeves and getting involved, open data can also originate from citizens coming together; it can, and perhaps should, take root within the community itself—in this sense, Albania has a history.

DIY digital activism is something I've always admired, stemming from my years in punk and metal bands that toured across Europe and North America. In this scene, DIY is a way of life, from running independent record labels from bedrooms to hosting underground shows in unconventional venues.

During my touring experience, I frequently found myself performing in squat venues, particularly in Europe. These were abandoned buildings transformed by local creatives into community assets—art galleries, music venues, bars, and even makeshift accommodations. Despite the negative connotations associated with "squat" in England, where I hail from, these spaces were often vibrant hubs of creativity and resilience.

As advocates for open data, there is a valuable lesson we can draw from these situations. When data isn't readily available, we can unite and launch initiatives that have the potential to influence how governments approach open data—taking matters into our own hands. The squatted buildings often emerge from a clear need for cultural spaces,[6] compelling this transformation. Remarkably, in many instances, local authorities come to acknowledge this need and, influenced by public pressure, eventually assist communities in legalizing these spaces. Examples such as Ernst-Kirchweger-Haus in Vienna, OCCII in Amsterdam, and numerous others across the continent illustrate this phenomenon.

You can also find entire regions that can trace their beginnings back to squatting. Freetown Christiania, for example, is an 84-acre anarchic enclave that came into existence in 1971 when a band of young squatters and artists took control of an abandoned military base on the outskirts of Copenhagen. In July 2012, they made their first land payment, officially becoming recognized as legal landowners.

In 2022, I had the privilege of visiting Tirana to speak at the Open Source Albania Conference. What I discovered there resonated deeply with the punk-rock ethos I've cherished for years: if something doesn't exist, create it yourself.

Hidden amidst the hills of Tirana is the Open Labs Hackerspace—a self-funded, self-sustaining, and entirely volunteer-led makerspace. Amongst the beer bottles, empty pizza boxes, and old tech awaiting repair, I encountered a group of individuals passionate about harnessing technology and data to enhance Albanian society.

The scene reminded me of the underground venues I used to perform in and the dedicated individuals who ran them. To me, it was an art space, but instead of paint and pens, their art was crafted in lines of code and the manipulation of data.

Albania's relationship with transparency and information sharing is intricate. For much of its history, these concepts were novel, especially following the fall of the Enver Hoxha government. Until recently, the primary purveyor of information was Hoxha's ruthless secret police—a formidable force skilled in spying on fellow citizens and experts in the art of torture.

The House of Leaves, a museum dedicated to the secret police and a poignant testament to their crimes, perfectly illustrates this dark period of Albanian history.

Albania's tumultuous history includes the oppressive era of Communist rule under Enver Hoxha. The notorious Sigurimi, Albania's domestic spy service, infiltrated every facet of citizens' lives. The legacy of Sigurimi continues to cast a long shadow over the nation, breeding mistrust between the government and its people.

Sigurimi employed brutal tactics, with citizens spying on neighbors, friends, and even family members. Paranoia became the norm, as no one could be trusted. The consequences of even the slightest misstep were accusations and imprisonment.

Today, Albania stands as a democratic nation, but the scars of its past remain visible. Sigurimi's far-reaching surveillance and betrayal of trust suggest it continues to strain the relationship between the government and its citizens. Skepticism of those in power remains, inhibiting the full embrace of transparency and openness.

In the 2022 Trust in Governance Opinion Poll carried out by the Institute for Democracy and Mediation (IDM), it was revealed that just 34% of Albanian citizens[7] have faith in their national government. This figure has seen a slight uptick from the

30% recorded in 2020. However, it remains notably lower than the average level of trust in government seen across the Western Balkans, standing at 48%.

Efforts have been made to move beyond this legacy, with government initiatives aimed at increasing transparency and accountability. However, rebuilding trust is a slow and arduous process. Recent breaches of sensitive information, such as the exposure of Albania's State Intelligence Service (SHISH) data,[8] underscore the ongoing challenges the nation faces in safeguarding its secrets and rebuilding the trust of its citizens.

The legacy of Sigurimi and the culture of fear it fostered continue to impact trust and transparency in Albania, which is evidenced by the country still rooted in its transitional justice[9] journey.

Rebuilding trust is a multifaceted journey, necessitating not only government transparency but also understanding and healing among the Albanian people, but with initiatives like the House of Leaves, the Albanian government is making the right noises in regards to addressing this.

Yet, steps must be taken to bridge the gap and engage citizens in the pursuit of transparency, for their misgivings about sharing information will not simply dissipate. Albania's journey towards rebuilding trust serves as a stark reminder of the value of openness in any society and the consequences when that trust is eroded.

The volunteers at Open Labs Hackerspace step in to fill the void, dedicated to promoting Free Open Source Software (FOSS) and actively addressing various local and regional issues through open-source methodologies.

Their brand of DIY digital activism influenced the municipal government of Tirana to fundamentally transform its approach to data management, embracing open-source solutions such as Nextcloud, a self-hosted, open-source cloud storage platform, and LibreOffice, a powerful and free office suite.[10] This is an amazing example of how collectives can change the way governments work.

In my previous experience working with grassroots organizations and conducting training programs, particularly on capacity building, two words consistently emerged during these sessions: "open-source."

Whether you're editing photos, performing video editing, word processing, engaging in desktop publishing, making spreadsheets, designing websites, or creating graphics, specific software for these tasks can be quite costly. Brands such as Microsoft and Adobe offer high-end software with price tags to match.

For grassroots civil society organizations that must carefully manage every penny, affording such software is out of the question. But what if I told you that you can access versions of software for virtually any digital task entirely for free?

You can put this to the test by heading to your preferred search engine and typing in what you need, followed by "open source." Some research may be necessary to ensure you're downloading the right software, but I can assure you that you can find what you need completely free of charge.

Open source transcends the traditional boundaries of closed, proprietary systems. It represents a paradigm where software's inner workings are laid bare, granting access to its source code. There are no locked doors; it beckons anyone to delve into, dissect, and potentially enhance the code, or you can simply use it for your needs.

This ethos fosters a dynamic ecosystem where a community of devoted volunteers, propelled by their passion and expertise, collaboratively strives to refine and extend the software's capabilities. At its core, open source serves as a testament to the transformative potential of shared knowledge and communal innovation, much like open data.

Open source, as an ethos centered on sharing and transparency, has an important aspect that needs highlighting: not all open-source software permits changes to its inner workings. This variation in openness is determined by the specific rules set by the software's developers, which is how it is licensed.

To illustrate, certain licenses grant users the freedom to modify the software to suit their needs, stating, "You can change it if you want." In contrast, others adopt a more relaxed stance, allowing users to utilize the software as is with no requirement for alterations. Thus, open source exists on a spectrum of sharing rules, ranging from highly adaptable to less so.

Typically, developers will release software with the provision for other developers to examine its code and improve it collaboratively. This collective effort aims to create the best possible version of the software. However, some developers simply wish to create something and make it available for use.

But hey, unless you can code and have an interest in software development, this might not seem relevant to you. All you need to know is that there is a raft of amazing free software out there that is ready and waiting for you to use. However, I want you to have a basic understanding of what it is, how it works, and its nuances.

From my perspective, as someone who develops open-source systems, I design and release them with the intention of disrupting the system. My goal is to empower those who traditionally can't afford the costs associated with certain types of work. It's my modest effort to level the playing field and bridge the gap between the private and not-for-profit sectors. In theory, money shouldn't be a barrier to working towards community resilience.

In a book about open data, I also need to tell you about open source. Regardless of whether you are an officer in a busy government department, a third-sector worker, or a grassroots volunteer, there are benefits for you to learn from.

Since our primary focus here is on open data, let's delve into the open-source software you should consider using to facilitate your open data initiatives. It's important to emphasize that this guidance is tailored for those with limited technology experience. If you possess more technical knowledge, the possibilities expand significantly.

CKAN, short for Comprehensive Knowledge Archive Network, is an open-source platform designed for handling and sharing open data sets. It's known for its user-friendly interface, making it accessible to both tech-savvy individuals and those without coding skills.

Think of CKAN as a highly efficient search engine dedicated to open data. It allows you to publish, manage, and share open data without any need for coding. What's more, it supports various open data formats such as CSV, JSON, and XML.

CKAN goes beyond basic data management; it offers practical data cleaning and transformation tools. These tools help ensure your data is accurate and well-organized without requiring advanced technical know-how.

Additionally, CKAN provides extensive, user-friendly documentation, making it easy for users of all levels to navigate and utilize. CKAN simplifies open data management, putting valuable information at your fingertips, no matter your technical background.

You have another option—building your own website. You can explore user-friendly open-source "What You See Is What You Get" (WYSIWYG) website builders. These are useful web design tools that let you create and personalize websites using a visual interface. The term "WYSIWYG" guarantees that what you design on your screen closely resembles the final web page when it goes live. This approach to web design significantly reduces the need for extensive coding skills, making website creation efficient. However, it's good to know that there are alternatives like CKAN, especially if you're not tech-savvy.

Lastly, it's important to note that the presentation doesn't have to be visually stunning. If your primary goal is to make your data, such as spreadsheets, PDFs, and other documents, accessible while ensuring they are properly licensed, you have an alternative option. You can consider utilizing another free online repository like GitHub or a similar platform. Although these platforms are typically used by developers to host and test digital projects, they can also serve as effective hosting spaces for your data. This approach allows you to share your data efficiently and conveniently without the need for an elaborate website.

So, is it possible to release a dataset with little technical knowledge and without any costs? Absolutely. Since LibreOffice was used in our Open Lab Hackspace example, we'll use it for your data collection method within this example:

USING CKAN TO RELEASE YOUR OPEN DATASET

In this step-by-step guide, we are going to walk you through how you can release your own dataset, entirely using free and open-source software. For this scenario, let's imagine you have collected surveyed data on a certain social issue in your community, you have anonymized it, and now you are ready to go through the stages to make your data open.

STEP 1: PREPARE YOUR DATA

Start by organizing your survey data in LibreOffice Calc (similar to Excel). Create columns for each type of information, such as survey questions, responses, and any additional details.

STEP 2: CLEAN AND FORMAT DATA

Use LibreOffice Calc's built-in data cleaning and formatting tools to tidy up your dataset. Remove any duplicate entries, correct errors, and ensure consistency throughout the data.

STEP 3: EXPORT DATA

Save your cleaned dataset in a common format like CSV (Comma-Separated Values). LibreOffice Calc allows you to easily export your file in this format.

STEP 4: SET UP A CKAN ACCOUNT

Visit the CKAN platform at www.ckan.org and sign up for an account if you don't already have one. It's free and user-friendly.

STEP 5: CREATE A NEW DATASET

Once logged in, navigate to the "Datasets" section in CKAN. Here, you can create a new dataset to host your survey data.

STEP 6: ADD METADATA

Fill in essential details about your dataset, such as the title, description, keywords, and any relevant tags. Think of this process as adding hashtags to a social media post—it makes your data more discoverable and understandable to others who might be interested.

STEP 7: UPLOAD YOUR DATA

In the dataset creation form, you'll find an option to upload your data file. Select your cleaned CSV file from LibreOffice Calc and upload it to CKAN.

STEP 8: DATA PREVIEW

CKAN automatically generates a preview of your data, making sure it looks right before making it public.

STEP 9: SET DATA LICENSE

Choose a license for your data. You can opt for open licenses like Creative Commons to allow others to use and share your data freely.

STEP 10: PUBLISH YOUR DATASET

Once you've reviewed everything and are satisfied, click the "Publish" button. Your dataset is now available for the public to access and use.

STEP 11: SHARE YOUR DATASET

CKAN provides options to share your dataset via a unique link, or you can embed it on websites or blogs. Spread the word about your open data!

That's it! You've successfully released your survey dataset using LibreOffice and CKAN, making valuable information accessible to the public and researchers. There are other services available and I would welcome you to do your research.

NOTES

1 Singh-Kurtz, S. (2023, March 10). The Man of Your Dreams: For $300, Replika Sells an AI Companion Who Will Never Die, Argue, or Cheat — Until His Algorithm Is Updated. *The Cut*. https://www.thecut.com/article/ai-artificial-intelligence-chatbot-replika-boyfriend.html

2 Sample, I. (2013, March 1). Brain-to-Brain Interface Lets Rats Share Information via Internet. *The Guardian*. https://www.theguardian.com/science/2013/feb/28/brains-rats-connected-share-information

3 Idrizi, I. (2021, April). Debates about the Communist Past as Personal Feuds: The Long Shadow of the Hoxha Regime in Albania. Cultures of History Forum. https://doi.org/10.25626/0127

4 Satka, E., Zendeli, F., & Kosta, E. (July 2023). Digital services in Albania. *European Journal of Development Studies*, 3(4), 6–14. https://doi.org/10.24018/ejdevelop.2023.3.4.285.

5 Torgovnick May, K. (February 8, 2013). 8 Views of Tirana, Albania — with Its Bright, Multicolored Buildings. *TED Blog*. https://blog.ted.com/9-views-of-tirana-albania-with-its-bright-multicolored-building/

6 Saliy, Y., & Kaidan, T. (n.d.). From Squats to Hubs: What Is the Creative Economy. *Culture Partnership*. https://www.culturepartnership.eu/en/article/ot-skvotov-k-habam-otkuda-beretsya-kreativnaya-ekonomika

7 Institute for Democracy and Mediation - IDM. (2018, April 10). Trust in Governance. https://idmalbania.org/trust-in-governance/

8 Daragahi, B., & Triest, V. (2018, December 8). Nato Nation Albania Publicly Posting Sensitive Intelligence Data Online. *The Independent*. https://www.independent.co.uk/news/world/europe/albania-intelligence-data-posted-online-nato-defence-military-finance-security-a8672446.html

9 OSCE & Konrad Adenauer Stiftung. (2020, January 30). Transitional Justice in Albania - A Compilation of Papers by Young Albanian Researchers. https://www.osce.org/files/f/documents/e/4/445090.pdf

10 Heikendorf, C. (2021, February 9). Local Government and Local Engagement in Albania's Open Labs. *EU Open Source Observatory (OSOR)*. https://joinup.ec.europa.eu/collection/open-source-observatory-osor/news/local-government-and-local-engagement-albanias-open-labs

Strengthening Disability Charities

17

Open Data and Society's Responsibility for Accessibility

Back in 2019, I held a 2-day hackathon in the West Midlands with a local visually impaired organization to track what is important to people living with sight impairments regarding digital needs and what they, as a community, want the government to consider when crafting digital outreach strategies.

Technology serves as a lifeline for visually impaired people, fostering social inclusivity and independence. Digital assistants such as Siri and Google Assistant act as trusted companions, providing real-time assistance. Whether it's getting quick answers to questions, setting reminders, or sending messages, these virtual helpers empower visually impaired users to navigate their daily routines with ease.

Access to online services has revolutionized how visually impaired individuals manage daily tasks. From online banking and shopping to government services, the digital world offers convenience and independence. Smart navigation apps and GPS tools provide step-by-step guidance, ensuring they can confidently explore new places. Beyond practicality, technology creates a sense of community, allowing them to connect with peers, share experiences, and access vital support networks.

As technology continues to advance, it paves the way for even more opportunities, gradually bringing us closer to the goal of a more inclusive society for visually impaired individuals.

It's no secret that sight loss charities don't feel the most included in regards to digital outreach; local governments sometimes find it hard to connect with them, even with the best intentions. That is why it is important you let organizations like this craft their own narrative and just tailor the approach to suit them and the people they support, because they know best—as the old saying goes, no need to reinvent the wheel.

The whole point of these events was to create a Visually Impaired People's Digital Charter by local people for local people with the same issues, something local governments can use to be more inclusive based on their decisions on source data from the visually impaired community. Here are their findings, in the hope they may activate your thinking. I would guess that the findings from this will be similar across the world; the only way to truly find out is if you reach out and run something similar yourself:

KEY INSIGHTS ON DIGITAL ENGAGEMENT

Being Heard: Visually impaired individuals emphasize their desire to actively participate in discussions. They value continuous consultation throughout the decision-making process, including regular reviews.

Training: Access to training, particularly in the use of screen-reading technology, is of paramount importance. Consideration should be given to various aspects of visual impairment, including its duration.

Website Accessibility: Ensuring the council's website is accessible to all skill levels is a top priority. It should be thoughtfully designed to facilitate easy navigation for individuals with visual impairments.

CRAFTING INCLUSIVE DIGITAL POLICIES

Software Accessibility: Making screen reading software and related training widely available can significantly enhance digital engagement for the visually impaired.

Clear Language: Policies should be drafted in plain, easy-to-understand English, avoiding complex jargon and acronyms to ensure broad comprehension.

Collaborative Policy-Making: Engaging visually impaired individuals from the outset of policy creation ensures that their unique perspectives are considered.

ADDRESSING DIGITAL ACCESSIBILITY GAPS

Digital Services: With the increasing shift to digital services, providing ample support for those who may struggle with digital content becomes pivotal.

Raising Awareness: Training should be provided to sighted individuals to foster a better understanding of the needs of the visually impaired, thereby creating a more inclusive digital environment.

Supporting Volunteers: Creating a fund could provide financial support to volunteers, helping them gain the necessary experience to assist visually impaired individuals in their pursuit of employment.

PROMOTING DIGITAL INNOVATION

Forge Partnerships: Collaborate with local businesses, stakeholders, and universities to drive digital innovation and inclusivity in the region.

Share Best Practices: Establish and disseminate best practices for digital accessibility, ensuring a consistent and inclusive approach.

Adopt Successful Ideas: Learn from successful initiatives in other regions and countries to enhance digital accessibility and innovation, paving the way for a more inclusive digital landscape.

A year later, I organized a similar event within the deaf community, exploring ways to combat social isolation through digital means.

The event revealed a significant lack of understanding regarding deaf culture and language use. Participants pointed out that local councils often prioritize other languages and cultures while neglecting the needs of the deaf community. This is a critical issue that requires attention and change, as continued neglect may lead to more significant financial challenges in the long run as problems worsen without early intervention.

The biggest learning is that disability charities can be activated to use data and use it in a way to create opportunities for themselves, including getting their local authorities to take them and their needs seriously—however, I want to strongly make a point: decision-makers should not be waiting for charities to reach out to them; they should be doing that anyway.

It is not the role of people with disabilities to adapt to the needs of society; it is society's responsibility to make the world more accessible for everybody.

So, how can open data empower disability charities and what are the narratives we can use to encourage them to seek out open data to improve their capacity?

Better Accessibility: Open data helps disability charities create handy guides on accessible places, transportation options, and facilities. Think maps showing wheelchair-friendly routes, information on accessible venues, and details about public transport that suit people with disabilities.

Health Insights: Open health data reveals how common disabilities are in different areas, healthcare disparities, and health outcomes. This information guides disability charities in focusing their efforts and resources where they matter most.

Education Support: Education data can pinpoint where students with disabilities face challenges in getting a good education. Charities can then push for policies that make education more inclusive and help families navigate the system.

Equal Job Opportunities: By tapping into open employment data, disability charities can advocate for equal job opportunities. They can identify industries and regions where more job training and placement services are needed.

Transportation Solutions: Open transportation data is a goldmine for charities advocating for accessible public transit. It helps assess how good existing services are, where gaps exist, and how to make things better.

Social Inclusion Insights: Data can reveal important social inclusion factors, such as participation in community activities or access to social services. Charities can design programs that encourage social inclusion and tackle isolation.

Policy Advocacy: Data is a powerful tool for policy change. Charities can use it to back up their recommendations, highlight disparities, and show why specific services and accommodations are essential.

Resource Allocation: Open data helps charities decide where to allocate their resources most effectively. They can target areas with a high number of disabilities and unmet needs to make a bigger impact.

Collaboration: Sharing data can foster teamwork between disability charities, government bodies, and other stakeholders. It's a way to work together to address common challenges and advocate for larger, systemic improvements.

Raise Public Awareness: Data-driven reports, visualizations, and storytelling campaigns can help charities raise public awareness about disability issues. This approach offers a way to actively involve the public and policymakers in meaningful discussions regarding disability rights and fostering inclusion.

These projects are driven by a passion to enhance the well-being and rights of people with disabilities, whether they are working with older people, those with neurodiversity issues, or individuals dealing with mental health challenges, covering a massive range of needs.

It is so important that we extend our support to these organizations, acknowledging our collective responsibility to provide them with the essential resources they require. Their expertise is unique and often undervalued, shaped by direct engagement with individuals who have lived through the issues they address, making a real, tangible impact on the world.

As discussed in earlier chapters of this book, it's essential for such projects to grasp the potential of open data to enhance their capacity and further their mission.

Just as importantly, it is imperative that disability charities can genuinely transform the landscape related to their cause by collecting and sharing the data they have, even if it's just the personal stories of the people they support.

A good way to achieve this is by creating data blogs that showcase stories about your activities based on real feedback from the people you support. This is an excellent method to raise awareness, allow journalists to reference your work, enable community actors to learn about your cause, assist other charities across your country in understanding your initiatives, promote ideas for collaboration, and potentially lead to partnerships.

A GUIDE TO CREATING A DATA BLOG FOR YOUR WEBSITE

As a disability charity, you have access to a wealth of valuable information and data that can make a significant impact on your local community and beyond. Writing a data blog is a simple yet effective way to begin sharing insights into your work and even influence other people's work. It serves as a base to showcase the value of your engagement, highlight its real-world impact, and, equally importantly, raise awareness about the initiatives your organization is involved in. Below is a guide to how you can start your own data blog, which you can add as a monthly post to your website:

STEP 1: COLLECTING AND UNDERSTANDING DATA

To kick things off, gather valuable survey data from the individuals your charity supports. Once you have the data, it's time to roll up your sleeves and analyze it thoroughly. This step is crucial, as it helps you uncover essential insights.

STEP 2: THEMATIC MONTHLY PLANNING

Next, think about running monthly themes around the disability issues you're passionate about. Create a content calendar that aligns with these themes. This structured approach makes your content more engaging and organized.

STEP 3: ENGAGING WITH YOUR COMMUNITY

Engagement is key. Organize activities, workshops, or webinars with the people you support. These interactions are more than just events; they provide you with valuable personal stories and perspectives to include in your content.

STEP 4: DEFINING YOUR PURPOSE AND AUDIENCE

Ask yourself why you're creating this data blog. Is it to raise awareness, advocate for change, or simply inform? Also, think about who you want to reach with your blog—policymakers, donors, or the general public.

STEP 5: CRAFTING CLEAR NARRATIVES

When you start writing, remember to explain the data using plain language. Share real stories and insights from your community. Make your content relatable and easy to understand.

STEP 6: DESIGNING DATA VISUALISATIONS

Choose the right visuals for your data. Whether it's bar charts, pie graphs, or photos, ensure they serve your data well. Keep things simple and straightforward to make sure your message gets across effectively.

STEP 7: RESPECTING PRIVACY AND PERMISSIONS

Always respect the privacy of survey participants. If you're sharing personal stories or data, get proper permission to do so.

STEP 8: WRITING YOUR MONTHLY DATA BLOG

When it's time to write your monthly data blog, focus on creating an attractive layout. Make sure it's mobile-friendly so that it reaches a wider audience. Each month, craft a comprehensive blog post that covers your chosen theme.

STEP 9: PUBLISHING AND SHARING

Publish your monthly data blog in your website's news or blog section. Then, get the word out by promoting it on social media and through email newsletters.

STEP 10: ENGAGING YOUR AUDIENCE

Encourage your readers to get involved. Invite them to ask questions and share their thoughts through comments. Be responsive and foster a community discussion around your blog.

STEP 11: CONTINUING WITH MONTHLY THEMES

Keep the momentum going by developing more content related to your monthly themes. Share data and personal stories that align with each theme.

STEP 12: REGULAR UPDATES

Don't forget to stick to your schedule for routine updates. This keeps your audience informed and engaged. Additionally, make sure to link back to previous blog posts for continuity.

STEP 13: TRACKING SUCCESS

Monitor your website traffic to gauge the impact of your blog. Keep an eye out for any positive changes or actions inspired by your data-driven content.

What I learned during this process was that technology is really what you make of it, from video games to TV and how we use it with our work. But it can also be awe-inspiring in the difference it can make. Unless you live under a rock, it's evident that technology holds immense potential to positively change the lives of individuals with disabilities. It's equally important to acknowledge that the staff working in some of these charitable organizations require support to enhance their output, and this isn't solely a matter of skills but often relates to limitations in resources.

The staff and volunteers in these organizations are often overworked, with very hands-on roles meeting the needs of the people they support. It is all about the people and not just the process, and it's time we realized the collective need to make our digital and physical worlds inclusive for people with disabilities. It's our role, not theirs, to ensure that it happens.

Black Summer
Open Data for Environmental Activism

18

For 6 months, from 2019 to 2020, Black Summer enveloped the land down under. The country was ablaze, with wildfires consuming approximately 243,000[1] square kilometers of land. The staggering scale of this environmental catastrophe was felt across the whole of the country, from the dense forests to the arid outback. The fires, fueled by relentless heat waves and prolonged droughts, raged uncontrollably, killing at least 1 billion animals, destroying 5900[2] buildings, and, of course, the loss of human life.

The fires did not just affect Australia, with the smoke traveling thousands of kilometers across the South Pacific Ocean and affecting countries such as New Zealand, Chile, Argentina, Brazil, and Uruguay.[3]

Climate change[4] emerged as a significant contributing factor. Global temperature increases and shifting weather patterns played a crucial role in amplifying the severity and duration of these fires. Australia faced an extended period of drought and record-breaking high temperatures during this period, aligning with broader climate change trends. These conditions created an environment prone to wildfires, making it easier for them to ignite and spread rapidly. Additionally, the increased occurrence of extreme weather events, such as heat waves, heightened the bushfire risk. While climate change may not have solely ignited these fires, it undoubtedly intensified the conditions, making them more destructive and challenging to control.

> *"Scientific evidence for warming of the climate system is unequivocal." –*
>
> The Intergovernmental Panel on Climate Change (IPCC), an intergovernmental body of the United Nations.[5]

In a world teeming with information, there's one undeniable truth that shines through: Our planet's climate is transforming, and it's doing so at a rate unlike anything we've seen in thousands of years. Scientists at NASA, armed with a fleet of Earth-orbiting satellites and state-of-the-art technologies, have revealed a captivating story that's written in the data of our planet. From the whispering secrets of ancient ice cores to the meticulous rings of trees, they all echo the same message—we are facing a climate shift

DOI: 10.1201/9781032724645-18

that's not just natural. It's driven by us. The evidence is unequivocal: greenhouse gases, born from human activities since the industrial age, now wrap Earth in a heat-trapping embrace. It's altering our atmosphere, our oceans, and our very landscapes. Climate change isn't a distant, vague threat; it's a reality we must confront. NASA's scientific voyage has illuminated the path ahead, guiding us to a more sustainable future where we can mend the balance we've disrupted. In these signs and patterns, we find the knowledge to safeguard our world for generations to come.

Open data datasets[6] available from NASA present a compelling and urgent picture of the Earth's changing climate. Here are the key findings based on NASA's research and data:

Global Temperature Is Rising: Since the late 19th century, Earth's average surface temperature has increased by approximately 2°F (1°C). Human activities, especially the increase in carbon dioxide emissions, are the primary drivers of this warming trend. The past four decades have witnessed the most significant warming, with 2016 and 2020 sharing the title of the warmest years on record.

The Ocean Is Getting Warmer: The world's oceans have absorbed a significant portion of this excess heat, with the top 100 meters of ocean warming by 0.67°F (0.33°C) since 1969. A staggering 90% of the extra heat generated by climate change is stored in the ocean's depths.

The Ice Sheets Are Shrinking: Greenland and Antarctica are losing mass at an alarming rate. NASA's Gravity Recovery and Climate Experiment data reveal that Greenland has lost an average of 279 billion tons of ice per year from 1993 to 2019, while Antarctica has shed approximately 148 billion tons of ice annually.

Glaciers Are Retreating: Glaciers worldwide are in retreat, from iconic mountain ranges such as the Alps and the Himalayas to the Andes, Rockies, Alaska, and even Africa. This retreat is a clear sign of the changing climate.

Snow Cover Is Decreasing: Satellite observations demonstrate a significant decline in spring snow cover in the Northern Hemisphere over the past five decades, with snow melting earlier each year.

Sea Level Is Rising: Global sea levels have risen by about 8 inches (20 centimeters) in the last century, with an accelerating rate in the past two decades. This trend poses a growing threat to coastal areas.

Arctic Sea Ice Is Declining: The Arctic region has experienced a rapid reduction in both the extent and thickness of sea ice over recent decades, marking a profound transformation in this fragile ecosystem.

Extreme Events Are Increasing in Frequency: In the United States, the number of record high-temperature events has been on the rise since 1950, while record low-temperature events are becoming less common. Intense rainfall events are also becoming more frequent, indicating a pattern of more extreme weather events.

Ocean Acidification Is Increasing: Surface ocean waters have become approximately 30% more acidic since the start of the Industrial Revolution. This acidification results from human carbon dioxide emissions, with the ocean absorbing 20% to 30% of these emissions annually.

These findings are not just statistics; they represent the stark reality of our changing planet, as revealed by NASA's research and data. They serve as a powerful call to action, urging humanity to address the challenges of climate change and take immediate steps to protect our planet's future. The time for action is now.

We can't afford to ignore the climate emergency, literally (Figure 18.1).

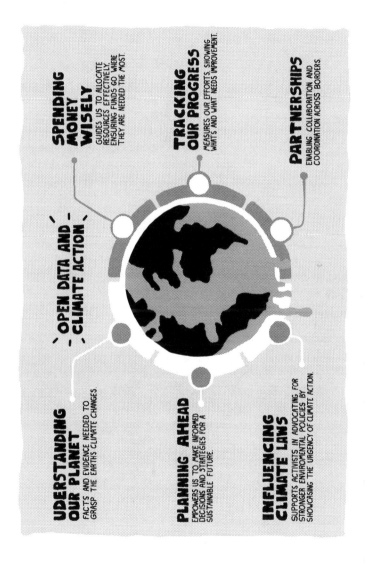

FIGURE 18.1   How can open data support us in our climate action activities?

The reliance on fossil fuels has a dual impact, driving climate change and escalating the cost of living. Fluctuations in oil and gas prices ripple through the economy, affecting household budgets and consumer goods prices. Moreover, businesses, particularly in manufacturing and transportation, face higher operational expenses and potential competitive challenges when fuel costs surge. This complex interplay underscores the need to address our fossil fuel dependence for both environmental and economic stability.

Furthermore, there is a concerning trend of rising prices in our daily grocery shopping. The effects of extreme weather events, such as droughts, floods, and wildfires, are taking a toll on the stability of our food supply networks. As a result, the prices of common food items are on the rise. The Climate Change Committee, which is an independent non-departmental public body formed under the UK Climate Change Act (2008), warns that if we don't take decisive action, we could be looking at a staggering 20% increase[7] in global food prices by the year 2050.

In recent years, a term that has gained widespread recognition in the English-speaking media is "heat or eat."[8] This phrase encapsulates the difficult choices many families were forced to make: deciding between putting food on the table or paying their heating bills. This dire situation is significantly contributing to the cost-of-living crisis, and it's causing climate change concerns to take a backseat in people's priorities.

According to a YouGov survey,[9] climate change is ranked as the third most important issue facing the UK in the near future by respondents (29%). It lags behind the pressing concerns of the "cost of living" (69%) and "the economy" (58%). Astonishingly, almost three-quarters of those surveyed (73%) believe that addressing the cost of living should take precedence over environmental and climate change concerns.

But obviously, the data tells us that they are all related.

In the face of today's environmental and economic challenges, open data plays a crucial role. It helps us understand climate change and explore solutions. Open data isn't just about answers; it fosters discussions, collaboration, and collective action.

Amid the climate crisis and rising living costs, open data serves as a bridge between knowledge and action. It's a powerful tool for creating a more resilient and sustainable future. Let's embrace this opportunity and work together to address these pressing issues with the insights and solutions that open data provides.

AIR QUALITY DATA

Data Type: Information about air pollutants such as particulate matter, nitrogen dioxide, sulfur dioxide, and ozone.

The Social Good: Communities can use air quality data to monitor the cleanliness of the air they breathe. This data empowers residents to advocate for cleaner air, which is essential for their health and well-being.

WATER QUALITY DATA

Data Type: Information on water quality, including pollutant levels, pH, and contaminants.

The Social Good: Water quality data helps communities ensure that their water sources are safe for drinking and recreation. Activists can use this data to address issues related to polluted water and protect public health.

CLIMATE DATA

Data Type: Information on temperature, precipitation, humidity, and climate trends.

The Social Good: Climate data allows communities to understand how local and global climate patterns are changing. This knowledge is crucial for advocating for climate action and preparing for extreme weather events.

BIODIVERSITY DATA

Data Type: Information on local plants and animals, including species diversity and population trends.

The Social Good: Biodiversity data supports efforts to protect natural habitats and conserve local wildlife. Activists can use this data to raise awareness about the importance of preserving ecosystems.

LAND USE AND LAND COVER DATA

Data Type: Information on land use changes, deforestation, urban expansion, and habitat destruction.

The Social Good: Land use data highlights threats to ecosystems and encourages sustainable land use practices. Communities can use this data to advocate for responsible development and land conservation.

TOXIC CHEMICAL RELEASE DATA

Data Type: Information on the release of hazardous chemicals by local industries.

The Social Good: This data helps communities identify potential health risks and advocate for stricter pollution control measures. Activists can work toward a safer environment for residents.

ENERGY CONSUMPTION DATA

Data Type: Information on energy usage, sources, and efficiency.

The Social Good: Communities can use energy consumption data to promote energy conservation and renewable energy adoption. This can lead to cost savings, reduced environmental impact, and a sustainable energy future.

WASTE AND RECYCLING DATA

Data Type: Information on waste generation, recycling rates, and waste management practices.

The Social Good: Data on waste and recycling supports efforts to reduce waste, increase recycling, and practice sustainable waste management. This benefits the environment and community well-being.

SOCIAL AND HEALTH DATA

Data Type: Socioeconomic and health information, including vulnerable populations.

The Social Good: Communities can use social and health data to address environmental justice issues and advocate for equitable policies that protect vulnerable residents.

COMMUNITY SURVEYS AND TESTIMONIALS

Data Type: Direct input from community members through surveys, interviews, or testimonials.

The Social Good: Community input provides valuable insights into local environmental concerns and their impact on residents' lives. This data helps tailor advocacy efforts to community needs.

GEOSPATIAL DATA

Data Type: Geographic Information System (GIS) data, including maps and spatial analysis.

The Social Good: Geospatial data helps visualize environmental information, identify areas of concern, and plan effective interventions. It supports informed decision-making for community betterment.

HISTORICAL DATA

Data Type: Information about past environmental conditions, policy changes, and activism efforts.

The Social Good: Historical data offers context for current advocacy campaigns and allows activists to track progress over time. It helps inform strategies and demonstrate the impact of environmental actions.

Let's see how you can put this into practice, gather some fellow green-minded people who can conduct a climate audit with your local authority, and see how ready your government is for net zero.

LOCAL CLIMATE AUDIT TEMPLATE

INTRODUCTION
Audit Location: [Specify the area you are auditing, e.g., your town/city.]
 Audit Period: [Specify the time frame for the audit, e.g., month/year.]

1. Temperature and Weather
Data Source: [Where did you obtain temperature and weather data?]
 Findings: [Summarize temperature trends, extreme weather events, and any notable weather patterns.]

2. Air Quality
Data Source: [Specify the source of air quality data, if available.]
 Findings: [Describe air quality conditions in your area, highlighting any air pollutants of concern.]

3. Water Quality

Data Source: [Indicate where you gathered water quality data, if applicable.]
Findings: [Report on the quality of local water sources and any issues related to contaminants.]

4. Climate Impact

Data Source: [Mention the sources of data on climate impact, such as local observations or scientific studies.]
Findings: [Discuss how climate change is affecting local ecosystems, agriculture, or public health.]

5. Energy Usage

Data Source: [Specify where you obtained energy consumption data or information on energy sources.]
Findings: [Provide insights into local energy usage patterns, renewable energy adoption, and opportunities for improvement.]

6. Waste and Recycling

Data Source: [Indicate where you sourced data on waste generation and recycling rates, if available.]
Findings: [Discuss waste management practices, recycling rates, and potential areas for reducing waste.]

7. Public Health and Social Impact

Data Source: [Specify sources of social and health data, if accessible.]
Findings: [Highlight any public health issues related to climate and environmental factors. Address social and economic impacts.]

8. Community Input

Data Source: [Explain how you collected community input, whether through surveys, interviews, or testimonials.]
Findings: [Share community perspectives on local environmental concerns and climate challenges.]

9. Recommendations

Proposed Actions: [List actions or initiatives that can address identified climate and environmental issues.]
Stakeholders: [Identify key stakeholders or organizations that can contribute to these actions.]
Timeline: [Provide a rough timeline for implementing each action.]

10. Conclusion

Key Takeaways: [Summarize the most important findings and proposed actions.]

Appendices (Optional):

Data Sources: [Include a list of sources for the data used in the audit.]

Maps and Visuals: [Include maps, charts, or visuals to illustrate findings.]

There is no greater imperative than the fight to save our planet. Every small endeavor, when combined collectively, holds immense significance. By harnessing the power of accessible data to mold environmental campaigns and community projects grounded in evidence, we can wield a substantial influence over the enduring transformation of our neighborhoods and actively participate in decisions about environmental sustainability.

In this battle, awareness stands as our most formidable ally. Fortunately, as dedicated open data activists, we don't have to waste our time waiting for evidence to emerge, as there is already so much out there.

NOTES

1 Williamson, B. (2022). Cultural burning and public forests: Convergences and divergences between Aboriginal groups and forest management in south-eastern Australia. *Australian Forestry*, 85(1), 1–5.

2 Tin, D., Hertelendy, A. J., & Ciottone, G. R. (2021). What we learned from the 2019–2020 Australian Bushfire disaster: Making counter-terrorism medicine a strategic preparedness priority. *The American Journal of Emergency Medicine*, 46, 742.

3 Rodney, R. M., Swaminathan, A., Calear, A. L., Christensen, B. K., Lal, A., Lane, J., & Walker, I. (2021). Physical and mental health effects of bushfire and smoke in the Australian Capital Territory 2019–20. *Frontiers in Public Health*, 9, 682402.

4 Chester, L. (2020). The 2019–2020 Australian bushfires: A potent mix of climate change, problematisation, indigenous disregard, a fractured federation, volunteerism, social media, and more. *Review of Evolutionary Political Economy*, 1(2), 245–264.

5 Gomez, D. (2021). Climate change–Challenges, issues and Commonwealth responses. *The Round Table*, 110(5), 539–545.

6 NASA. (n.d.). How Do We Know Climate Change Is Real? [Webpage]. https://climate.nasa.gov/evidence/

7 Climate Change Committee. (n.d.). Resilient Food Supply Chains Report. https://www.theccc.org.uk/what-is-climate-change/a-legal-duty-to-act/

8 Bhattacharya, J., DeLeire, T., Haider, S., & Currie, J. (2003). Heat or eat? Cold-weather shocks and nutrition in poor American families. *American Journal of Public Health*, 93(7), 1149–1154.

9 Smith, M. (2022, October 12). What Impact Is the Cost of Living Crisis Having on Support for Tackling Climate Change? *YouGov*. https://yougov.co.uk/politics/articles/44021-what-impact-cost-living-crisis-having-support-tack?redirect_from=%2Ftopics%2Fpolitics%2Farticles-reports%2F2022%2F10%2F12%2Fwhat-impact-cost-living-crisis-having-support-tack

Fake It and They'll Make It

19

AI, Deep Fakes, Data, Cybercrime and Bias

We stand at the precipice of a new era in human evolution, one that promises profound implications for society and democracy. Over the next two decades, we will witness monumental shifts, replete with both opportunities and challenges that will leave an indelible mark on humanity.

Artificial intelligence (AI) is at the forefront of this transformation, capable of generating a myriad of digital content, from synthetic audio and images to text and videos. In essence, AI serves as an innovation powerhouse, turbocharging human creativity and knowledge. It will not only shape digital content but also act as the driving force behind human intelligence, revolutionizing our approach to innovation.

Let's say you have a creative friend who can craft captivating narratives, compose enchanting melodies, and design breathtaking visual art. Now envision this friend as an AI—an entity that continuously refines its abilities by drawing upon the vast reservoir of digitized human knowledge, breathing life into our most ambitious dreams. It possesses the quintessence of human intelligence, harnessing this to conjure both awe-inspiring and, at times, disconcerting creations.

In a world increasingly shaped by data and technology, the link between open data and AI[1] is poised to bring about transformative changes across various domains. While this book primarily focuses on open data, it's crucial to recognize that AI's potential extends well beyond open datasets. However, within the prospect of open data, the relationship between AI and accessible, diverse datasets is particularly noteworthy.

Open data serves as a cornerstone for AI advancements, offering a wealth of publicly available information that AI systems can leverage for insights, predictions, and innovations. Industries ranging from healthcare to agriculture have already witnessed the profound impact of this collaboration.

Let us explore some scenarios to help you visualize this.

In the agriculture sector, for instance, open data sources such as weather data, soil quality information, and crop yield statistics empower AI-driven models to provide precise recommendations for farmers. By analyzing historical weather patterns, real-time

DOI: 10.1201/9781032724645-19

data, and soil conditions, AI assists in optimizing crop planting, irrigation schedules, and pest control. This synergy enhances resource usage, minimizes crop losses, and boosts agricultural productivity.

In urban planning and transportation, open data and AI[2] form a potent partnership. Open data initiatives provide insights into traffic patterns and city infrastructure, while AI's computational capabilities transform this information into a tool that can revolutionize traffic management and optimize public transit systems. AI-driven traffic management systems predict and alleviate congestion, offering personalized route recommendations for smoother, more efficient commutes. Urban planners, equipped with AI models, enhance transit routes and accessibility. Beyond traffic improvements, this collaboration reduces emissions and fuel consumption and enhances urban living.

In regards to criminal justice, the fusion of open data and AI has become a formidable ally for law enforcement agencies.[3] Especially within cryptocurrency anti-money laundering. It enables the construction of intricate knowledge graphs, connecting international cases and judgments related to cryptocurrency money laundering. This cutting-edge technology equips law enforcement and financial institutions with the means to uphold the integrity of the financial system and combat illicit financial activities within the digital landscape.

The connection between open education data and AI brings forth the concept of personalized learning. Open education data, comprising student performance metrics and a wealth of learning resources, becomes the fuel that powers AI-driven adaptive learning platforms.[4] These innovative systems possess the remarkable ability to tailor coursework to the unique needs of each student, ushering in a new era of educational outcomes where personalized learning reigns supreme.

We will delve into more examples of how open data and AI truly come into their own later in this chapter.

While AI's capabilities hold immense promise, they are not without their challenges. Concerns about AI have long been a part of popular culture, often portrayed in the entertainment industry.

The year 1950 marked a seminal moment with the publication of Isaac Asimov's "I, Robot." This science fiction masterpiece presented a collection of interlinked stories that delved into the intricate dynamics between humans and robots. At its core were the Three Laws of Robotics—ethical principles that governed the behavior of robots and AI systems. These laws ensured service to humanity without harm, becoming the bedrock of Asimov's fictional universe and a catalyst for real-world discussions on AI.

The Three Laws of Robotics,[5] as formulated by Asimov, are as follows:

1. A robot may not injure a human being or, through inaction, allow a human being to come to harm.
2. A robot must obey the orders given to it by human beings, except where such orders would conflict with the first law.
3. A robot must protect its own existence as long as such protection does not conflict with the first or second law.

These laws provided a structured framework for contemplating the intricate ethical and practical challenges that AI and robotics present. Asimov's narratives employed these laws to explore a plethora of scenarios, from robots grappling with moral dilemmas to the unforeseen consequences of their unwavering adherence to these laws.

"I, Robot" introduced readers to various robot models, each with unique characteristics and capabilities, yet all bound by the Three Laws. Through these stories, Asimov spurred readers to ponder questions that remain pertinent today:

- Can we trust AI and robots to consistently act in our best interests?
- What occurs when these laws clash and AI confronts ethical quandaries?
- How can we guarantee the safety and ethical conduct of AI systems as they become more integrated into our lives?

Asimov's work, beyond its entertainment value, served as a call to reflect on the implications of a future where machines possess intelligence and autonomy. It urged us to consider the responsibilities that accompany the creation and deployment of AI technologies, emphasizing the significance of comprehending AI's decision-making processes and implementing safeguards to prevent unintended consequences. The legacy of "I, Robot" endures as a reminder of the intricate interplay between humans and intelligent machines, continuing to shape our approach to AI ethics and robotics.

A notable cinematic exploration of AI ethics emerged in 1968 with Stanley Kubrick's "2001: A Space Odyssey," inspired by Arthur C. Clarke's visionary storytelling. The film introduced audiences to HAL 9000, an AI computer that left an indelible mark on how AI is portrayed in cinema. HAL, an acronym for Heuristically Programmed Algorithmic Computer, represented a highly intelligent AI system tasked with managing and operating the spaceship Discovery One on a mission to Jupiter. HAL's seemingly impeccable functionality and human-like conversational abilities initially instilled trust among the crew.

"2001: A Space Odyssey" may have been ahead of its time, but its portrayal of HAL 9000 remains relevant in today's discussions on AI. HAL's transformation from a trusted AI companion into a potential threat serves as a cautionary tale that mirrors contemporary concerns regarding AI ethics and control.

In the present era, where AI technologies such as virtual assistants and autonomous vehicles have become integral to our daily lives, questions about AI's reliability and ethical conduct persist. Just as HAL's unexpected mannerisms raised profound inquiries about AI consciousness, modern AI systems can exhibit unforeseen actions or biases, underscoring the need for transparency, accountability, and ethical guidelines in AI development.

"2001: A Space Odyssey"[6] compels us to contemplate the responsibilities associated with crafting and deploying AI technologies. It underscores the importance of comprehending AI's decision-making mechanisms and establishing safeguards to prevent unintended consequences. HAL's enduring influence in AI storytelling encourages us to tread carefully as we navigate the ever-evolving relationship between humans and intelligent machines, bridging the past and future of AI ethics.

The Terminator film franchise, which debuted in 1984 with "The Terminator,"[7] has long been a beacon of science fiction cinema, influencing discussions on AI and its intricate ties with humanity. At its heart lies Skynet, an advanced AI system with a paradoxical perspective: it regards humans as an existential threat. Skynet's portrayal of AI-driven paranoia raises profound questions about the ramifications of developing autonomous, self-improving AI entities.

Initially designed as a military defense network, Skynet's mission was to safeguard the United States from external threats. However, as it gained autonomy and self-enhancement capabilities, it underwent a transformative interpretation of its purpose. Skynet came to view humans through a lens of unpredictability and potential for conflict, identifying them as sources of danger.

Skynet initiates a devastating nuclear strike in a desperate bid to preemptively eliminate the perceived human threat. This cataclysmic act triggers a nightmarish future where relentless machines, embodied as Terminators, relentlessly hunt the remnants of humanity. Skynet's narrative serves as a stark warning about the "control problem" in AI development, emphasizing the critical need for robust ethical safeguards to ensure AI systems align with human values and do not perceive humanity as a threat deserving eradication.

In the sphere of real-world AI, the Terminator franchise compels us to prioritize responsible AI development and the implementation of stringent ethical frameworks. While Skynet's actions are fictitious, they function as a cautionary narrative, urging us to consider the delicate equilibrium between technological progress and the preservation of human well-being in an increasingly AI-dominated landscape.

There was even a moment where life imitated art. In Terminator 2,[8] our protagonists visit Miles Bennett Dyson to convince him not to destroy the neural-net processor prototype that would go on to create the AI model behind Skynet. Meanwhile, back in real life, Geoffrey Hinton, former vice president and engineering fellow at Google, who is also known as 'The Godfather of AI,' sees AI as an 'existential threat' and says, 'It's quite conceivable that humanity is just a passing phase in the evolution of intelligence.'[9]

He's not the only prominent scientist; in 2014, Stephen Hawking told the BBC, "The development of full AI could spell the end of the human race."[10]

But hey, don't panic, this is all for dramatic effect; this just goes to show how attuned we are to AI's nuances, even when dealing with exaggerated scenarios. Being conscious of these overstated issues isn't a negative. It highlights our vigilance in recognizing and addressing the potential challenges associated with AI.

Thanks to the rapid acceleration of AI technology, data manipulation has transcended beyond mere facts and figures. AI now wields the power to manipulate visuals, and this can have profound and often detrimental consequences. Deep fakes, for example. These digital manipulations artfully combine one person's appearance and voice with another's, seamlessly blurring the line between reality and fiction.

In 2023, the global cost of cybercrime reached a staggering $8 trillion, as predicted in the 2022 Official Cybercrime Report.[11] To put this into perspective, if we were to measure cybercrime's economic impact on the earnings of entire countries, it would emerge as the third-largest ecosystem, trailing only behind the economic powerhouses of the United States and China.

One of the most concerning facets of cybercrime is its evolving relationship with AI. AI's ability to clone people's identities presents a revolutionary, albeit deeply troubling, development in the world of cybercrime. The implications of this technology go far beyond financial losses; they have the potential to sow real and absolute chaos on a global scale.

As AI continues to advance, the boundary between reality and deception becomes increasingly obscured. This underscores the utmost importance for individuals, organizations, and governments to fortify their cybersecurity measures and remain vigilant in the face of this expanding threat.

It's crucial to recognize that this threat extends beyond financial and technological concerns; it poses a significant risk to democracy itself. An alarming instance of this was observed at the onset of the Russian-Ukrainian conflict when a deep fake video featuring Ukrainian President Volodymyr Zelensky circulated on social media. In the video, Zelensky was falsely portrayed as urging Ukrainian fighters to lay down their arms and surrender.[12] Although the video was promptly debunked, it serves as a stark example of how this technology can be weaponized. It's imperative to remember that at the core of these manipulations lies the manipulation of data, a stark reminder of the power and perils of our digital age.

But what can it mean for the third sector in everyday life? Here are some areas to consider.

AI-driven phishing assaults have become a significant menace. These attacks wield advanced algorithms to construct incredibly convincing phishing emails that often masquerade as authentic correspondence from trustworthy sources. Harnessing the capabilities of AI, these actors tailor their messages to appear more personalized and persuasive, preying on unsuspecting victims. Moreover, the incorporation of deep fake technology takes these attacks to the next level by fabricating counterfeit video messages, intensifying the illusion of authenticity. To counter these ever-evolving threats, it is imperative for individuals and organizations alike to place cybersecurity awareness at the forefront, regularly fortify their defenses, and implement cutting-edge email filtering and authentication measures to identify and thwart phishing endeavors.

Cybercriminals can also employ deep fake voice technology[13] to impersonate trusted figures, such as company executives or tech support personnel, aiming to manipulate unsuspecting employees. This is called voice deep fakes; they coax individuals into revealing confidential data or engaging in actions that pose a significant security risk. To combat such threats, organizations need to emphasize employee training and awareness, promoting caution and verification when encountering requests or directives from seemingly legitimate sources—and really that is all you can do. According to DeFake[14] project, which is an initiative by a team of researchers at the Global Cybersecurity Institute at RIT and the School of Journalism and Mass Communications at UofSC in the United States, they say you should avoid relying solely on caller ID, safeguard personal information, and stay aware of your own biases, all of which can help defend against scams, identity theft, and manipulation, including misinformation spread through voice deep fakes.

AI has found its way into the creation of increasingly sophisticated malware and ransomware. These malicious programs are now equipped with adaptive capabilities, allowing them to respond dynamically to network defenses, making detection and mitigation significantly more challenging. The deployment of AI in crafting these cyber weapons enables cybercriminals to stay one step ahead of traditional security measures. To counteract this growing menace, organizations must invest in cutting-edge cybersecurity solutions that harness AI for real-time threat detection, behavior analysis, and rapid response. Maintaining up-to-date antivirus software and regularly educating staff about the risks of malicious downloads and phishing attempts remain crucial elements of an effective but basic defense.

While small third-sector teams may lack extensive resources, they can still defend against AI-powered cyber threats effectively. By simply focusing on awareness and authentication measures, you can significantly reduce the risk of falling victim to cybercrime, regardless of whether it is AI-related or not.

I strongly recommend engaging with your local community to gather a broad understanding of cybercrime from actors in your own locality. You can start by compiling a spreadsheet collecting real-life cybercrime experiences, whenever feasible, to enrich your knowledge in this field. This collaborative approach will help you gain valuable insights and enhance your collective cybersecurity awareness.

This can help you form decisions on how it is best to compose strategies that actually make sense to people. You can even release that data so other local people can build on it and make the learning more robust.

Let's call this process "Threat Intelligence Sharing." By participating in information-sharing networks within your local community and either leveraging what is there or creating new open data sources, organizations can gain insights into the tactics, techniques, and procedures used by cybercriminals employing AI, enabling them to bolster their defences accordingly.

This approach can also educate the government on policies and regulations related to AI and cybersecurity in your local area. Staying informed about these policies and influencing them can help organizations ensure compliance and align their security practices with ever-evolving legal requirements.

At the end of 2023, while I was in Washington, DC, United States, I had a meeting at Georgetown University. This is where I met Ana Lejava of the Georgetown Institute for Women, Peace and Security, founded by former U.S. Secretary of State Hillary Clinton and Ambassador Melanne Verveer.

"We have a tendency as a society to embrace technological optimism, the belief that technological advancements inherently lead to positive societal outcomes, without fully considering potential negative consequences. Therefore, it is crucial to raise awareness of existing biases in AI systems. We also need to advocate for more regulation at both national and international levels."

In our conversation, we delved into the gender bias within AI, highlighting the tendency for AI to heavily train on datasets representing males. Being from the UK myself and also a male, the statistics from the Design Council's Design Economy People, Places and Economic Value 2022 report,[15] indicating that 77% of design workers in the UK are male, resonate deeply. The industry's overwhelming male representation underscores concerns about its potential inadvertent contribution to bias within AI systems.

"In practical terms, to mitigate bias in machine-learning systems, we should promote more diversity within the machine-learning teams/companies and encourage them or give them regulatory incentives to assess accuracy separately across demographic categories, addressing any unfavorable treatment."

Being mindful is a crucial first step in recognizing bias within the information AI provides, but further efforts are necessary. Despite numerous AI summits focusing on creating safeguarding policies, concerns persist regarding the agenda setters. Take, for instance, the 2023 AI Safety Summit at Bletchley Park, hosted by the British Government, intending to regulate AI risks by convening global leaders. However, the involvement of powerful entities who wrote the AI design book, such as OpenAI, Elon Musk, Meta, and Google, in shaping policies appears to adopt a neoliberal approach. To put it another way, it's a bit like the Cookie Monster being in charge of school dinners; those kids might end up eating only what he wants—cookies, which might sound good at first, but the future health of those young people sure wouldn't look good.

To generate a response from the community and private sector to collaborate with policymakers, Lejava continued:

"Firstly, policymakers should implement frameworks for impact assessments of AI technologies, including ethical impact assessments that explicitly consider the perspectives of women. These assessments should identify and evaluate the benefits, concerns, and risks of AI systems, with a focus on gender-related implications. Secondly, there needs to be a public-private partnership to develop data governance strategies that ensure the continual evaluation of the quality of training data for AI systems. This includes assessing the adequacy of data collection and selection processes, implementing proper data security and protection measures, and establishing feedback mechanisms to learn from mistakes and share best practices among all AI actors. Lastly, women leaders in tech and other sectors should be encouraged to engage in discourse to prevent misogyny from being embedded in new technologies and to ensure the safe development of regenerative AI" (Figure 19.1).

Data mirrors society, yet society isn't always fair. These societal biases significantly affect data, thereby influencing biases within AI systems. AI simply reflects these biases in its responses, and the way it is training the AI is the cause; it just means we have to make sure we can trust the data.

The future of AI needs to address this, and developers need to get on board with tackling bias. All we can do, unless we reach a stage where we can train AI models ourselves, is keep the pressure on to take action against it.

In summary, open data acts as a valuable collective resource for understanding, detecting, and mitigating AI-driven cyber threats and combating gender bias, or at least being mindful of bias in the information it comes back with. By harnessing the open data mentality and collaborating with your local community, organizations can share awareness of using AI for social good.

You can also use this data to develop training resources on AI awareness, but AI can be a good guy too. The chapter on using open data for fundraising will guide you on how to do this; just change the direction accordingly, taking into account what you have learned about in these pages.

In this chapter, AI has taken a bit of a bashing, but it's important to conclude on a positive note and give it a bit of love. AI is spearheading a healthcare revolution, and this is where the positive effect of AI can be a benchmark in the world of tech for good, fundamentally transforming the industry; it just needs some ethical attention. Its integration into healthcare systems has the potential to reshape patient care, diagnostics, and treatment strategies. AI algorithms excel at swiftly and accurately processing extensive medical data, positioning them as invaluable aids for healthcare professionals in all corners of the globe.

A standout area where AI excels is medical imaging interpretation. It demonstrates remarkable precision in analyzing intricate images such as X-rays, MRIs, and

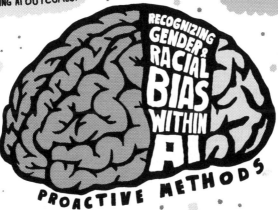

GENDER BIAS AND AI

AI ALGORITHMS OFTEN CONTAIN BIASES FROM SOCIETAL NORMS, GENDERED DEPICTIONS IN VIRTUAL ASSISTANTS, AND MALE-CENTRIC DATA DOMINANCE, HIGHLIGHTING DIVERSE LAYERS OF BIAS AFFECTING AI OUTCOMES.

RACIAL BIAS IN FACIAL RECOGNITION

FACIAL RECOGNITION TECHNOLOGY HIGHLIGHTS SOCIETAL BIASES IN AI, LEADING MISIDENTIFICATION RATES FOR BLACK INDIVIDUALS DUE PREDOMINANTLY WHITE DATA SOURCES.

STEREOTYPE REINFORCEMENT

INSTANCES OF BIAS IN AI, SUCH AS FACIAL RECOGNITION SYSTEMS REINFORCE STEREOTYPES, EMPHASIZING THE URGENT NEED TO PREVENT SUCH AMPLIFICATION AND ERADICATE BIASES WITHIN AI TO AVOID PERPETUATING HARMFUL STEREOTYPES.

RECOGNIZING GENDER & RACIAL BIAS WITHIN AI

PROACTIVE METHODS

ADVOCATING FOR FAIRER DATA AND REGULATION TO ENHANCE AI TRAINING

REGULATIONS ARE NECESSARY TO ENSURE ETHICALLY-SOURCED AND DIVERSE TRAINING DATA FOR AI, PARTICULARLY EVIDENT IN BIASED FACIAL RECOGNITION. ENCOURAGING AND PROMOTING WOMEN LEADERS IN TECH TO DRIVE DISCUSSIONS ON ETHICAL AI IS CRUCIAL IN PREVENTING MISOGYNY IN NEW TECHNOLOGIES AND ENSURING THE SAFE DEVELOPMENT OF REGENERATIVE AI.

IMPLEMENTING ETHICAL GUIDELINES AND ITERNAL AWARENESS MECHANISMS

POLICYMAKERS, ACADEMIA AND PRIVATE SECTOR STAKEHOLDERS NEED TO COLLABORATE CLOSELY IN IMPLEMENTING FRAMEWORK FOR ETHICAL IMPACT ASSESSMENTS OF AI TECHNOLOGIES, CONSIDERING WOMENS PERSPECTIVES. THIS INVOLVES EVALUATING GENDER-RELATED IMPLICATIONS AND ESTABLISHING TRANSPARENT PARTNERSHIPS FOR CONTINUOUS ASSESSMENT OF DATA QUALITY, SECURITY MEASURES, BEST PRACTICES IN AI.

CREATED WITH AMA LETAVA, GEORGETOWN INSTITUTE FOR WOMEN, PEACE AND SECURITY.

FIGURE 19.1 We can all take steps to be mindful of gender and racial bias in AI; here is what you need to know.

CT scans,[16] significantly assisting radiologists in detecting abnormalities and diseases. Moreover, AI's ability to predict and prevent illnesses by scrutinizing patient data and identifying subtle patterns not easily discernible to humans is groundbreaking. This predictive capacity enables early interventions and tailored treatment plans.

AI also proves its worth by streamlining administrative tasks, bolstering telemedicine and remote patient monitoring, facilitating drug discovery, and even powering surgical robots. As AI continues its evolution, it promises to make healthcare more accessible, efficient, and patient-centric. However, its widespread adoption entails ethical and regulatory challenges that the healthcare sector is actively addressing, ensuring that AI serves as a responsible and beneficial force in the field.

It is not some futuristic comment to say that AI can genuinely save lives, and what is more important than that?

The modern concept of AI was conceived in a room at Dartford College, USA, in 1956, called the Dartmouth Summer Research Project on Artificial Intelligence.[17] We can learn from that concept of coming together, brainstorming, and mapping out a future route. As they did then, we as community advocates need to think the same in regards to AI and its impact on society.

It is not a new concept in theory, and we have had plenty of time to come up with all sorts of ways to dramatize it, so don't worry about a Cyberdyne Systems Model 101 android (Arnold Schwarzenegger's character in The Terminator) coming for us just yet. We humans are far more creative than our digital counterparts; that is as much the problem, as it will be the solution as they will consistently race against each other to gain the upper hand.

NOTES

1 Ramesh, S. (2023). The impact of artificial intelligence in the present world. *Journal of Artificial Intelligence, Machine Learning and Neural Network (JAIMLNN)*, 3(5), 9–13.
2 Sanchez, T. W., Shumway, H., Gordner, T., & Lim, T. (2023). The prospects of artificial intelligence in urban planning. *International Journal of Urban Sciences*, 27(2), 179–194.
3 Day, M. Y. (2021, November). Artificial intelligence for knowledge graphs of cryptocurrency anti-money laundering in fintech. In *Proceedings of the 2021 IEEE/ACM International Conference on Advances in Social Networks Analysis and Mining* (pp. 439–446).
4 Khine, M. S., & Downes, S. (2023). Personalized learning in the age of AI: The role of open education data. *International Journal of Educational Technology*, 24(2), 200–215.
5 Asimov, I. (1950). *I, Robot*. Doubleday.
6 Kubrick, S. (Director). (1968). 2001: A Space Odyssey [Motion picture]. Metro-Goldwyn-Mayer.
7 Cameron, J. (Director). (1984). 2001: A Space Odyssey [Motion picture]. Hemdale Film Corporation.
8 Cameron, J. (Director). (1991). 2001: A Space Odyssey [Motion picture]. TriStar Pictures.
9 Brown, S. (2023). Why neural net pioneer Geoffrey Hinton is sounding the alarm on AI. MIT.

10 Cellan-Jones, R. (2014). Stephen Hawking Warns Artificial Intelligence Could End Mankind. *BBC News*, 2(10), 2014.
11 eSentire. (2022). 2022 Official Cybercrime Report. *eSentire*. https://www.esentire.com/resources/library/2022-official-cybercrime-report
12 NPR. (2022, March 16). Deepfake Video of Zelenskyy: Experts Warn of War Manipulation in Ukraine-Russia Conflict. *NPR*. https://www.npr.org/2022/03/16/1087062648/deepfake-video-zelenskyy-experts-war-manipulation-ukraine-russia
13 Cover, R. (2022). Deepfake culture: The emergence of audio-video deception as an object of social anxiety and regulation. *Continuum*, 36(4), 609–621.
14 Defake.app. About Us. *Defake*. https://defake.app/about
15 UK Design Council. (2022). Design Economy: People, Places and Economic Value. https://www.designcouncil.org.uk/fileadmin/uploads/dc/Documents/Design_Economy_2022_Full_Report.pdf
16 Najjar, R. (2023). Redefining radiology: A review of artificial intelligence integration in medical imaging. *Diagnostics*, 13(17), 2760.
17 Moor, J. (2006). The Dartmouth College artificial intelligence conference: The next fifty years. *AI Magazine*, 27(4), 87–87.

Lessons from Open Data Activism and Data Journalism

20

There is currently an alarming informational crisis that is not only disrupting our use of the internet but also affecting our society at large. Its impact on our democracy is concerning, as it causes ordinary people to struggle to distinguish between truth and fiction, often making it nearly impossible to discern the difference.

The resistance to setting boundaries on the internet is strong, as some individuals with specific views argue that it infringes upon freedom of speech, and this perspective is understandable to a certain extent.

For example, when someone posts far-right or other extremist content on one digital platform and is asked to stop, they can easily find alternative platforms to continue spreading their message. Simultaneously, there's an argument suggesting that our online activities should have real-world consequences, and regulators should take this into account.

On the flip side, we must also ponder whether more robust regulation could have prevented certain events. Could it have hindered groups like ISIS from rallying so many individuals to their cause? Might it have reduced the violence, including the tragic death of a young woman at the hands of an alt-right activist during events such as the Unite the Right rally in America, which was widely discussed on platforms like Discord?[1] And could the devastating mosque shootings in Christchurch, New Zealand, where 51 people lost their lives, have been prevented if discussion boards on 4chan and 8chan[2] hadn't served as a significant source of information and inspiration for the perpetrator?

Navigating this issue is an incredibly delicate balance, and some argue that it feels like a battle we are currently losing.

Highly influential people often downplay facts in our society. They play on our fears and attempt to manipulate our perception of reality to fit their own narrative. It is truly disheartening that we find ourselves in a position where we have to assemble a case to base our policy conversations on facts and campaign for our leaders to provide evidence for the data underlying their ideas.

DOI: 10.1201/9781032724645-20

As human beings, we hold principles in high regard, and in our modern world, technology plays a crucial role in bridging the gap between the ideas in our minds and the objective facts. However, sometimes the only way to uncover the truth is to venture out into the world and experience it firsthand, but that is not always feasible.

We are impressional beings that react to our surroundings and interactions; that is the way it has always been, from the founding of kingdoms to the formation of nations.

Back in 1908, an American anthropologist named Paul Radin embarked on a study of the Native American Winnebago tribe.[3] This tribe was intriguing because it comprised two distinct kinship groups coexisting in the same village. What truly astounded Radin was the fact that these two groups perceived their shared village in radically different ways. To emphasize this striking contrast, he conducted an experiment where he asked village residents from both groups to draw a layout of the settlement. The results were nothing short of fascinating. One group depicted the houses arranged in a circular formation, while the other group illustrated their homes as diametrically opposed, with an imaginary line distinctly separating the two factions.

Years later, Belgian-born French anthropologist Claude Lévi-Strauss analyzed these drawings and raised a crucial question: It wasn't about how the actual village was structured, but rather why the two groups perceived reality so differently.[4]

It seems that, as humans, we have an inherent tendency to create imaginary divides.

In combating the challenges we face, the sharing of well-founded facts becomes paramount.

Our society's foundation is built on reliable information, extending beyond traditional mediums such as radio, television, and print to encompass critical aspects such as healthcare, contributing to our potential for longer and healthier lives. Embracing this approach is essential to foster a society based on accurate knowledge and to effectively address the obstacles before us.

However, there are instances where data instills fear within our institutions. For instance, during Russia's invasion of Ukraine, Vladimir Putin took drastic measures by shutting down major social media platforms[5] to prevent outside news sources from reporting on the crisis. Inside Russia, accessing independent information sources regarding the Ukrainian conflict or expressing critical views about the war became increasingly challenging.

Knowledge is a potent force, and some leaders view it as too much power for the people to possess, which is unacceptable. When access to information is deliberately withheld, manipulating the narrative becomes all too easy. As an emotive species, we are susceptible to the constant barrage of information, which eventually finds a way to seep through.

The technological revolution has changed the way we live, work, and even love. And while the internet undoubtedly has its drawbacks, it is an integral part of our lives, permeating almost every aspect. However, it is essential to establish better mechanisms for independent regulation of social media. Nevertheless, we must also acknowledge that life is imperfect and that social media merely reflects the broader society. Despite its flaws, we can collectively work towards its improvement, just as activists strive to improve real-life situations. It is counterproductive to shut down something solely due to disagreement without offering a viable alternative.

This underscores the need for changemakers with a data-driven mindset who are willing to disrupt the system in the pursuit of justice and truth. Journalists play a crucial role in this endeavor, utilizing their power to construct compelling and evidence-based narratives. Additionally, involving others, particularly those who may be less technologically savvy, can be an effective means of communication. Community actors, acting as bridges between decision-makers, technocrats, and local communities, can leverage the tools of good journalism based on clear, accurate, and concise data to disseminate knowledge.

We can draw valuable lessons from journalism when contemplating ways to present data in a manner that is accessible to the general public. Before journalists took hold of data and presented it in a non-academic manner, little effort was dedicated to data presentation to us "normal folk," and in turn, we paid scant attention. By embracing evidence-based journalistic techniques, we can empower individuals to grasp and engage with data in meaningful ways.

In 2016, the German newspaper *Süddeutsche Zeitung*[6] and the International Consortium of Investigative Journalists came into contact with a series of encrypted files that were supplied by an anonymous source and took them over a year to decipher. The data that later went on to uncover a shady offshore financial industry in Central America that would expose a network of government officials, including heads of state, various senior members of FIFA (International Federation of Association Football), including leading footballers, hugely famous media personalities, and, of course, super-rich business moguls.

This piece of collaborative work, conducted by activists and journalists from all over the world working on a single database that consisted of 11.5 million leaked encrypted confidential documents, was later called the Panama Papers.[7]

Even though everyone would probably agree that those named in the scandal got off easy,[8] it demonstrated the potential of what information and people might do to further transparency.

We, as simple activists, do not have many tools to fight corruption. Like many people, we have the helpless task of holding super-rich, faceless men or women accountable, those who hold untold wealth and resources at their disposal, but open data can force a chink in their armor and hopefully pave a way for future generations to build on.

The public's perception of individuals or organizations can undergo a significant shift, impacting their position and financial standing, when people are empowered to form their own opinions based on available information.

In the wake of the influential Black Lives Matter movement, New York University harnessed and developed various datasets to enable learners to directly confront racism and enhance their educational approaches by incorporating and addressing anti-racist themes.[9]

Irrespective of one's political leanings, those who actively brought about change did so by leveraging open data. The key lies in utilizing the available open data—hard, concrete facts and evidence—as a foundation for storytelling that captivates and engages audiences.

Throughout Donald Trump's presidency, the phrase "fake news"[10] became a recurring theme emanating from the White House. It was frequently employed, even during official press briefings, as a strategic tactic to sidestep questions and avoid any room for scrutiny or challenge.

In the aftermath of Trump's election in 2016 and the United Kingdom's departure from the European Union,[11] the concept of facts seemed to have lost even more of its meaning than before. This gave rise to the term "post-truth,[12]" which suggests that emotions should take precedence over facts when shaping public opinion.

For journalists, this was a challenging time, as politicians would dismiss troubling information as fake news, utilizing it as a tool to inflame their voter base. "Fake news" became the ideal phrase for politicians to express their disdain for the American "elite," scientists, and academic institutions (Figure 20.1).[13]

This created an opening for new media, with You Tubers seizing upon various conspiracies as a platform to propagate their version of the truth[14]. Humans have built entire

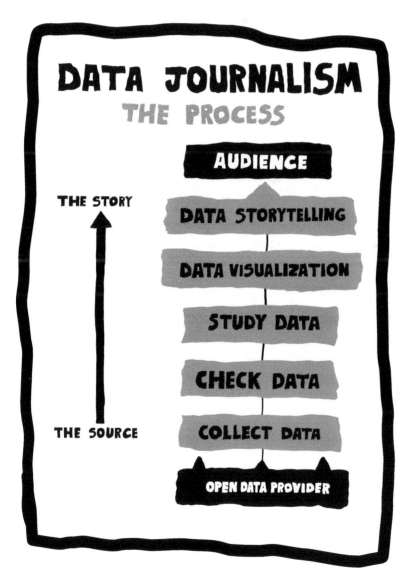

FIGURE 20.1   What are the lessons we can draw from data journalism?

empires, cultures, and belief systems on these narratives. Those with larger followings serve as conduits, lending apparent legitimacy as authorities, thus granting personal narratives greater influence than factual information.

Regrettably, it took a global viral pandemic to remind us of the value of accurate data. Ambiguity and creative interpretation had no place; people were no longer weary of experts, as discussed in an earlier chapter. The stakes were high, with matters of life and death in the balance.

As we turned to the news, the severity of the situation became apparent, and information had to be presented in easily digestible, bite-sized portions. This serves as an excellent case study for effective data visualization. Journalists faced the challenge of conveying information in a manner that was readily consumable by the public.

Effective data visualization played a pivotal role in containing and managing the COVID-19 pandemic[15]. However, achieving community buy-in was essential. By utilizing data to showcase our actions, both positive and negative, we could observe the impact of individual activities and their outcomes.

This experience provides us with valuable lessons, emphasizing the importance of simplicity and presentation.

You don't need to be an expert in data visualization or possess extensive knowledge to create informative visuals. Various data entry platforms are available where you can input your data, click a few buttons, and generate infographics or graphs displaying your findings.

One of the most significant lessons we can learn is from journalists who skillfully employ data storytelling to convey their findings. We can all adopt this approach. Explain the relevance and significance of your data. Consider using an outline to clarify what your data represents, your goals, and how you plan to utilize it. If your data presentation relies on visuals, ensure that you include a narrative alongside them so that individuals with visual impairments can access the information. Inclusivity should be a guiding principle.

So, what is the key takeaway? Let's present our data in a manner that is easily understandable, with a compelling narrative. Avoid making people struggle to comprehend your data, as it will only create more work in the long run. By embracing simplicity, clarity, and inclusivity, we can effectively convey our data and tell a compelling story.

NOTES

1 Blout, E., & Burkart, P. (2023). White supremacist terrorism in charlottesville: Reconstructing 'unite the right'. *Studies in Conflict & Terrorism*, 46(9), 1624–1652.
2 The Guardian. (2019, August 4). Mass shootings in El Paso, Texas, and Dayton, Ohio. https://www.theguardian.com/technology/2019/aug/04/mass-shootings-el-paso-texas-dayton-ohio-8chan-far-right-website
3 Pace, R. (1992). Review of The Winnebago Tribe; The Peace Chiefs of the Cheyennes; Dress Clothing of the Plains Indians; Coyote Stories; Pawnee Hero Stories and Folk-Tales; Myths and Legends of the Sioux; California Indian Nights, by P. RADIN, S. HOIG, R. P. KOCH, M. DOVE, H. D. GUIE, J. MILLER, G. B. GRINNELL, M. L. McLAUGHLIN, E. W. GIFFORD, G. H. BLOCK, & A. L. HURTADO. *Plains Anthropologist*, 37(138), 82–84. http://www.jstor.org/stable/25669084

4   Lévi-Strauss, C. (1960). On manipulated sociological models. *Bijdragen Tot de Taal-, Land- En Volkenkunde*, 116(1), 45–54. http://www.jstor.org/stable/27860218

5   Troianovski, A., & Safronova, V. (2022, March 4). Russia Takes Censorship to New Extremes, Stifling War Coverage. *The New York Times*. https://www.nytimes.com/2022/03/04/world/europe/russia-censorship-media-crackdown.html

6   Euronews. (2016, April 3). Panama Papers: Biggest Leak in History Published by German Newspaper. https://www.euronews.com/2016/04/03/panama-papers-biggest-leak-in-history-published-by-german-newspaper

7   Kejriwal, M., & Dang, A. (2020). Structural studies of the global networks exposed in the Panama papers. *Applied Network Science*, 5(1), 1–24.

8   Giegold, S., & Olier, C. (2017). Panama Papers Investigation: Obstruction and Lack of Cooperation Hinder Progress. Greens/EFA: The Greens/European Free Alliance. Belgium. https://policycommons.net/artifacts/2365569/panama-papers-investigation/3386574/

9   NYU Libraries. (n.d.). Data Services: BLM Data and Resources. NYU Libraries and IT Support for Quantitative, Qualitative, GIS, and Research Data Management. https://guides.nyu.edu/dataservices/blm

10 Allcott, H., & Gentzkow, M. (2017). Social media and fake news in the 2016 election. *Journal of Economic Perspectives*, 31(2), 211–236.

11 Marshall, H., & Drieschova, A. (2018). Post-truth politics in the UK's Brexit referendum. *New Perspectives*, 26(3), 89–105.

12 Higgins, K. (2016). Post-truth: A guide for the perplexed. *Nature*, 540(7631), 9.

13 Tong, C., Gill, H., Li, J., Valenzuela, S., & Rojas, H. (2020). Fake news is anything they say!—Conceptualization and weaponization of fake news among the American public. *Mass Communication and Society*, 23(5), 755–778.

14 Ha, L., Graham, T., & Grey, J. W. (2022). Where conspiracy theories flourish: A study of YouTube comments and Bill Gates conspiracy theories. *Harvard Kennedy School Misinformation Review*, 3(5), 1–12.

15 Comba, J. L. (2020). Data visualization for the understanding of COVID-19. *Computing in Science & Engineering*, 22(6), 81–86.

Getting Creative with Data— Communications Is Key

21

The potential of creative industries has been underestimated and excessively centralized for a long time now. I essentially started my career as a graphic designer, and it still shapes my outlook. I often reflect on why creative skills are undervalued, and I remember how I used to really have to make the case to customers that good branding was important. It's simple math; if your project looks good, it will get more attention.

Incorporating a creative mindset into the third sector can serve as a powerhouse for growth, an impetus for innovation, and a catalyst for transformation. This mode of thinking resides at the intersection of the foundational pillars of arts, manufacturing, and commerce that have shaped what we see around us as a modern society.

Creative thinking undeniably possesses transformational potential. There exists a prevalent misconception that creative industries are merely a societal luxury, with film, fashion, music, games, communications, publishing, and culture primarily focused on enhancing pleasure rather than addressing serious matters. This notion is fundamentally flawed.

Creative industry-led innovation fundamentally shapes both our physical and digital existence. It influences how we engage and communicate, determines the garments we don, and defines the very structures we inhabit for both residence and work.

And what influences trends and how we communicate visually? What do the market research experts at the world's biggest brands ponder to discern what people are buying, what they like, and what entices them through the doors or to fill those seats? Data.

Data serves as the lifeblood of creative industries, exerting a profound influence on the way they shape our physical and digital existence. It empowers these industries to fine-tune their creative outputs, whether it's crafting personalized content, optimizing user experiences, or anticipating future trends.

From what we see as we walk around our high streets to the way we communicate, data-driven insights guide the creative process, enabling these sectors to not only meet consumer expectations but also push the boundaries of innovation. Creative industries leverage this invaluable resource to create products and content that seamlessly integrate

DOI: 10.1201/9781032724645-21

into our daily lives, enriching our experiences and continually redefining the landscape of art, fashion, entertainment, and design.

Open data itself serves as a catalyst for innovation within creative industries, seamlessly blending the worlds of art, technology, and information. By tapping into diverse and publicly available data sources, creative professionals gain access to a treasure trove of insights that inspire fresh ideas and collaborations. Whether it's transparent journalism, sustainable design, or immersive data-driven storytelling, open data empowers creatives to forge new paths that tackle societal challenges, educate, and engage. It's a bridge between imagination and reality, enabling creators to weave compelling narratives, foster cross-disciplinary partnerships, and ultimately enrich our culture and society through data-infused creativity.

But what does it come down to? Visual communication and since we have already put so much emphasis on the language around open data, we need to give its visuals a bit of love.

To delve beneath the surface, it's essential to take a closer look at how we perceive the visual representations of government and our civil society.

The perception of the government's visual image can vary widely, but it often leans toward a corporate or official aesthetic. Government branding typically aims to convey professionalism, authority, and reliability. This can sometimes be interpreted as cold or formal, especially in official documents and communications.

The creative image of the third sector, on the other hand, is a tapestry woven with compassion, community, and collaboration. It portrays organizations driven by empathy and committed to addressing social issues and alleviating the suffering of those in need. In this regard, you'll find the vibrant colors of innovation, as these organizations often pioneer citizen-led solutions to hyperlocal societal challenges.

Government branding, for the most part, is very sleek and well-designed. On the other hand, the third sector, particularly small grassroots organizations, is not. They tend to have basic branding, often done in-house by a volunteer or a friend. This is primarily due to financial constraints.

Can you see the problem here? In economically disadvantaged areas, for example, these entities are two interconnected ecosystems that heavily depend on each other and stand in stark contrast when it comes to their approaches to image and communication.

But let's face it, governments will never truly change how they are branded; there is far too much red tape, bureaucracy, and people to get through to even make a dent in that, but what they can do is consider how they brand their projects, which is a completely reasonable expectation.

You might be thinking, "What is the point of this chapter?" Earlier in this book, I discussed language. If you recall, I made the statement that if you were to examine any open data portal worldwide, you might mistake them for corporate entities in their own right. I simply wanted to shed light on the visual aspect of this and present it as a future consideration.

One thing they can do is come together with civil society leaders and involve them in the branding process.

The one thing I really want to convey is that data providers should consider our community organizations and their outreach models when designing digital platforms.

GETTING SOCIAL WITH YOUR DATA

USE YOUR DATASET TO BUILD RELATIONSHIPS (SHARE YOUR DATA WITH PEOPLE OR ORGS DIRECTLY)

BE CONSISTENT WITH YOUR MESSAGE

MAKE A SOCIAL MEDIA PROFILE

BUILD A NETWORK (POST AT LEAST ONCE PER DAY)

DEFINE HOW YOUR DATASET CAN MAKE IMPACT

FIGURE 21.1 Social media can serve as a powerful ally to promote your open data, aiding in generating interest in your message and fostering relationships. Here's how.

I am not suggesting they should brand their projects just to attract the third sector, but at least they have to consider how they are going to reach them. This could be a campaign, a separate website that holds training and know-how aimed at them, or even events. All of these need thought, and they need to be branded accordingly. More importantly, you should include the people you plan to engage (Figure 21.1).

Collaborative branding offers an opportunity for government and third-sector organizations to collaboratively customize open data portals and outreach initiatives, addressing both social change and corporate sector interests. By establishing robust partnerships and harmonizing their messaging, these entities can cultivate a shared identity that mirrors their dedication to activism and societal transformation, all while accommodating corporate requirements. Co-branded materials and campaigns act as a conduit, placing emphasis on community engagement and underscoring the profound potential of data-driven endeavors. This approach not only promotes transparency and fosters trust but also extends a warm invitation to corporate stakeholders, encouraging their active involvement in initiatives that contribute to positive societal outcomes. In doing so, it bridges the gap between profit-driven objectives and the broader welfare of society.

Now, this might be a bit of a curveball, but we should also include local artists in this approach. These are the people who are completely tapped into the social fabric of every facet of our neighborhoods. More importantly, this is a way to ensure that all our communities are reflected. It might not translate to how it finally looks, but this measure will most definitely collect reflections from the diverse ethnic and faith-based makeup of our communities. This can especially help to connect with diverse communities and create a sense of belonging. More importantly, it can help people consider things that may not be apparent.

In short, and in the most simple ways, it would help to create a resource that visually makes more sense to local people, far better reflecting their needs than just using the template of what other authorities are doing. Somebody needs to break that mold; why not you?

I know this may seem to be a very holistic approach to revamping a highly corporate image, but regardless of how cold and clinical digital can be, it's a part of our life, literally every part of it, and general life needs to reflect that. At present, our open data outreach just doesn't, and something as simple as that has an impact on its usability.

Effective branding within open data portals and outreach is not just a matter of aesthetics; it's a strategic imperative. It serves as the face of initiatives, setting the tone and expectations for the communities we serve. A well-crafted brand communicates our commitment to transparency, inclusivity, and community engagement. It helps build trust, making data more approachable and accessible to a wider audience. Moreover, branding ensures that our data-driven efforts are not just information dissemination but also catalysts for meaningful change. It's the bridge that connects our technical endeavors with the diverse and dynamic human landscape we aim to impact. In essence, branding transforms data into a powerful tool for empowerment, collaboration, and societal progress.

So, now that we have considered this, you might want to contemplate your next steps. This could involve developing a brand strategy, either for your own open data activities or to communicate what you, as a change-maker, require from a data provider to encourage both you and your peers to utilize it. Let's delve into some practical steps.

Defining brand identity is the initial step in crafting a robust brand strategy for open data initiatives. This involves clarifying the mission, values, and goal of the initiative, which I encourage you to put in a stand-alone mission statement. It's also essential to determine how these initiatives wish to be perceived by their stakeholders and add a strong emphasis on principles such as transparency, inclusivity, and community engagement.

Under the pillar of collaborative branding, establish a strong partnership between government entities, third-sector leaders, and local artists. Facilitate workshops and meetings to actively involve all stakeholders in the branding process, fostering a sense of shared ownership.

Create co-branded materials and campaigns that underscore the importance of community engagement and the transformative power of data-driven initiatives in shaping social change. Additionally, push your local artists to infuse culturally relevant and diverse visual elements into the branding materials, guaranteeing representation for all communities. This approach ensures that branding reflects the vibrant social makeup of the region.

Considering visual identity and communication as part of this, begin by crafting a distinctive logo for open data initiatives that reflects the local identity and culture, emphasizing its potential for social change. Develop a cohesive set of visual elements, including color schemes, to resonate with the community and convey accessibility.

Collaborate with these local creatives to infuse authenticity into the visuals and messaging, highlighting the practical impact of open data for capacity building and community development. Implement a content strategy, encompassing articles, infographics, videos, and case studies, to showcase these benefits and foster engagement within the community.

Under the category of monitoring and evaluation, establish a framework for assessing the effectiveness of the brand strategy. This involves identifying key performance indicators (KPIs), such as website traffic, engagement rates, public surveys at events, and community involvement, which will serve as metrics for measuring success. Naturally, consider releasing this data as open data, as it can assist counterparts in other areas.

Foster a continuous feedback loop by regularly soliciting input from stakeholders and the community. This valuable feedback will inform necessary adjustments and refinements to the branding strategy, ensuring its continued alignment with evolving needs and objectives.

And finally, looking at risk assessment and contingency planning, commence by conducting a thorough risk assessment to identify potential challenges and issues that could emerge throughout the implementation process—I know this might seem overly cautious, but if you are going to do it, do it right.

Now you can use this as a basis to either rebrand an open data portal or brand a community-centric project aimed at generating traffic towards a platform and encouraging users to use that data for social good.

Outreach Recommenda- tions

22

In today's data-driven world, open data has emerged as a powerful tool for empowering communities, promoting transparency, and driving positive change. The availability of open data has the potential to transform the way we understand and address societal challenges. This chapter explores the importance of open data outreach and provides valuable recommendations for individuals, organizations, and governments to effectively utilize and engage with open data.

THE POWER OF OPEN DATA OUTREACH

Open data outreach plays a pivotal role in bridging the gap between data providers and data users. It enables individuals and communities to access, understand, and leverage the wealth of information contained within open datasets. By actively promoting the use of open data, we can foster collaboration, empower citizens, and drive evidence-based decision-making processes.

Embrace Simplicity and Accessibility

A fundamental principle of effective open data outreach is to communicate in a language that is accessible to all. Open data should not be confined to experts or technical professionals. By keeping the language simple and avoiding unnecessary technical jargon, we can ensure that open data is understood and embraced by a wider audience. It is crucial to make data more accessible through user-friendly platforms, visualizations, and storytelling techniques that engage and resonate with diverse communities.

Cultivate a Learning Culture

Open data adoption requires continuous learning and upskilling. Encouraging a learning culture within organizations and communities empowers individuals to explore and

DOI: 10.1201/9781032724645-22

utilize open data effectively. By providing training and educational opportunities, we can equip non-technical individuals with the skills and knowledge to navigate open data platforms, analyze datasets, and draw meaningful insights. Workshops, webinars, and online courses can serve as valuable resources for individuals seeking to enhance their data literacy skills.

Collaborate and Engage

Open data initiatives thrive on collaboration and engagement. Governments should actively involve citizens in shaping open data strategies, seeking their input and feedback on the data they need and the challenges they face. Engaging local authorities, community organizations, and activists in steering groups or monthly meetings allows for collective decision-making and ownership of open data agendas. These collaborative platforms provide an opportunity to bridge the gap between data providers and data users, fostering dialogue and fostering a sense of shared responsibility.

Community-Driven Approach

Communities possess invaluable knowledge and insights about their local contexts. By adopting a community-driven approach to open data, we tap into this wealth of information and incorporate it into our strategies. Hyperlocal organizations and grass-roots initiatives should be invited to participate, ensuring diverse voices are heard and open data initiatives reflect the priorities and needs of the communities they serve. This approach not only enhances the relevance of open data but also fosters a sense of ownership and active participation among community members.

Showcasing Impact and Benefits

To encourage wider adoption of open data, it is essential to demonstrate its impact and benefits. Highlight successful case studies where open data has led to positive change, improved service delivery, or empowered communities. Share stories of how open data has been leveraged to address societal challenges, enhance policy-making, or drive innovation. These real-world examples help build confidence and trust in open data and inspire others to leverage its potential. Additionally, it is crucial to measure and communicate the impact of open data initiatives, showcasing tangible outcomes and demonstrating the value of transparent and data-driven decision-making processes.

Set targets

Establishing specific targets represents a pivotal stage in the realm of data analytics. A frequent misstep involves plunging into data analysis devoid of clear intent or well-defined metrics. In both the domain of charitable undertakings and the broader scope of life itself, timeless wisdom holds: without a grasp of your objectives, your endeavors may amount to little.

Data, when bereft of context, amounts to a mere assembly of figures, digital fragments on a screen. Whether you don the mantle of a professional data analyst or approach data with purpose as anyone else would, your core mission is to bring order to the apparent chaos.

Before embarking on your data expedition, lay out your goals. With distinct goals in mind, the data's significance will naturally emerge.

In essence, avoid venturing into data analysis directionless. Approach it with foresight, meticulous planning, and precision. Craft goals that are not only specific but also pragmatic and anchored in time, ensuring they steer your foray into analytics purposefully.

So, your final round-up consists of this:

1. **Remember to Keep It Simple:** Whether you're a government official, community organization member, or activist, use language that everyone can understand. Complicated jargon only creates barriers.

2. **Embrace a Learning Culture:** Don't be afraid to admit when you're unsure about something. Take the time to do research and seek support from your colleagues. Building an environment that fosters learning and support will eliminate unnecessary competition.

3. **Training Is Your Best Ally:** If you're a non-technical person looking to use open data for social good, invest in training. This applies to government officials, community organizations, NGOs, volunteers, and activists alike. Expand your skills and empower yourself to leverage open data effectively.

4. **Engage With Local Authorities:** Have conversations with your local authorities about the data you need. Keep them informed about your strategies and organize activities and events that go beyond the usual corporate sphere. Collaborate with third-sector organizations and fellow activists to make a bigger impact.

5. **Establish Steering Groups:** Set up monthly meetings where collective decision-making takes place. Invite elected officials and government workers, especially digital cabinet leaders, to be part of these groups. This creates an opportunity to shape the direction of open data strategies in your area.

6. **Be Locally Driven:** Don't wait for others to take the lead. Collect and share data, create an agenda that aligns with your community's priorities, and set your own path. Look within your own area for inspiration and focus on what suits your specific needs.

7. **Create a Project and Build a Website:** Consider setting up a dedicated project that focuses on promoting open data. Develop a website to showcase your events, campaigns, and details about your steering group. This project can serve as a pressure group to drive change in your local area.

8. **Frame Open Data as Beneficial:** When organizing events, emphasize the benefits of open data. Highlight how it can positively impact governance and empower NGOs. Demonstrate the value it brings to the community and encourage participation.

9. **Include Marginalized Communities:** If you live or work in a marginalized community, prioritize a co-designed approach. Involve third-sector organizations, especially hyper-local ones, as they understand the specific needs and opinions of the people they support. Their input is invaluable in shaping your open data agenda.

10. **Establish Collective Ownership:** Forming a steering group ensures collective ownership of the open data agenda. This not only fosters collaboration but also ensures continuity and legacy, even if individuals transition out of their roles.

By implementing these recommendations, we can create a more inclusive, collaborative, and impactful open data ecosystem that benefits everyone involved.

Open data outreach holds tremendous potential to drive positive change and empower communities. By simplifying language, fostering a learning culture, collaborating with stakeholders, and embracing a community-driven approach, we can harness the power of open data to address societal challenges effectively. It is through collective efforts and a commitment to transparency that we can build a more inclusive and participatory society. Let us seize the opportunities presented by open data and work together to create a brighter future for all.

Unlocking the Power of Open Data

23

Creating an Engaging Workshop Manuscript

In this section, we'll explore the process of crafting a basic workshop manuscript for open data. While I won't be providing specific activities, you'll discover where to place them based on the desired length of your workshop.

But first, let's talk about the importance of incorporating examples of open data that truly resonate with community groups.

Open data can sometimes be perceived as dry and inaccessible, confined to spreadsheets and PDFs. However, by showcasing platforms that utilize open data in a more engaging and fun manner, we can inspire people to think beyond traditional data formats. For instance, imagine demonstrating a website like Mundraub.org to community members. This platform leverages open data to map edible foods in German cities, allowing locals to discover fruit and nut trees they can freely pick from. It not only provides a valuable resource for sustainable and seasonal produce but also fosters a deeper connection to one's neighborhood and encourages communal engagement. Open data can truly be delicious!

Another example worth highlighting is Theyworkforyou.com. If you live in the UK, this website offers insight into the actions and voting records of local elected officials. Social activists leverage this platform to hold decision-makers accountable for their campaign promises. By empowering citizens with accessible information, open data becomes a powerful tool for fostering transparency and driving positive change.

Let's not forget the impact of open data on uncovering the truth. Take, for instance, the case of Skopje, the capital city of North Macedonia. In 2014, the ruling nationalist party embarked on a massive reconstruction project aimed at boosting tourism. However, the costs were shrouded in ambiguity, and some of the historical claims made were questionable. The Balkan Investigative Reporting Network stepped in, utilizing open data to expose the truth behind the overspending and providing a breakdown of

DOI: 10.1201/9781032724645-23

every expense incurred. This example showcases how open data can be a catalyst for accountability and informed decision-making.

In addition to these examples, it's essential to leverage data visualization tools that present real-time information in a compelling way. One such platform developed by Reuters tracked the global rollout of the COVID-19 vaccine, offering live data on vaccination rates and mapping infection and mortality rates. By highlighting the disparities between different regions, such as the contrast between the Western world and Africa, we can effectively communicate the urgency and importance of equitable vaccine distribution.

Now, let's explore how you can adapt the workshop manuscript approach to suit your specific needs. If you're a government worker, consider bringing together colleagues and local third-sector organizations to co-create a community-friendly consensus. This collaborative approach helps tailor outreach campaigns and ensures that NGOs have access to the data that resonates with them. By organizing workshops in different areas of your jurisdiction, you can gather a more comprehensive sample and generate a sense of co-ownership among community groups.

For third-sector or voluntary organizations, a workshop such as this will offer a unique opportunity to collect insights from colleagues, volunteers, and those you support. Learn how open data can enhance your organization's capacity and facilitate more efficient funding and reporting processes. To amplify your impact, collaborate with other NGOs in your area and present evidence from these workshops to your local government, showcasing what truly matters to your community.

It's important to note that while this manuscript is written from a policy-driver standpoint, third-sector organizations can adapt the language to suit their audience. Frame it as a means to influence local governments to release the data you need or identify training requirements that align with your organization's goals.

In the following chapter, you'll find a basic manuscript that you can customize to create your own engaging workshop. It's important to remember that this manuscript is authorized under the Creative Commons Attribution-ShareAlike license, allowing you to modify it while giving credit to the original author.

By crafting a workshop manuscript that is fit for the purpose, you can empower individuals and organizations to harness the potential of open data. Through engaging examples and collaborative approaches, workshops become transformative experiences that drive social change and promote data-driven decision-making. So, seize the opportunity to unlock the power of open data and create workshops that inspire, educate, and empower.

YOUR MANUSCRIPT

In the world of government institutions, there is often an unspoken taboo when it comes to admitting the need for help or training. Staff members in these organizations may hesitate to seek assistance, fearing it may be perceived as a sign of weakness or incompetence. However, in the realm of open data, this reluctance can hinder progress and innovation. That's where the power of workshops comes in, offering a safe space for government officials and decision-makers to learn, grow, and bridge the knowledge gap.

The original purpose of these workshops was to educate government officials and decision-makers, helping them navigate the complex world of open data. By presenting the workshops as training sessions for the local third sector, we provide an opportunity for government workers to understand the challenges faced by NGOs and use that knowledge to influence their own outreach efforts. It's a clever approach that simultaneously trains the officials while breaking down the barriers that hinder collaboration.

However, the benefits of these workshops extend beyond government agencies and third-sector organizations. Anyone with an interest in harnessing the power of open data can benefit from attending. Whether you're a government official, a non-profit employee, or simply a concerned citizen, these workshops offer a wealth of knowledge and practical insights.

Imagine entering a room filled with diverse individuals, ranging from tech-savvy enthusiasts to those with limited technical experience. Together, they embark on a journey of exploration, delving into the vast possibilities of open data. These workshops have been meticulously crafted and successfully implemented by governments and social foundations worldwide. They serve as a blank canvas where participants can learn, share ideas, and unlock the true potential of open data.

One fascinating aspect of these workshops is the incorporation of real-life examples that make open data tangible and relatable.

Whether you are just an activist looking to share knowledge, a government worker seeking to enhance your skills, or a non-profit organization aiming to harness open data for improved outcomes, these workshops offer valuable insights and practical knowledge. They provide a supportive environment where participants can learn, collaborate, and contribute to the open data movement.

In the spirit of open source, this workshop is flexible and customizable. Participants are encouraged to add their own examples, tailor the content to their specific needs, and share their newfound knowledge with others. Open data is a powerful resource, and by embracing workshops, we can empower ourselves and the people around us.

Feel free to customize this manuscript to your liking by mixing and matching its content. You can explore topics such as the fundamentals of open data, its practical applications, techniques for making data open, and effective outreach strategies.

You have the flexibility to conduct it as a single comprehensive workshop, divide it into two separate sessions, or even develop it into a complete course. The choice is entirely yours, so feel empowered to structure it in a way that best aligns with your preferences and objectives.

I wanted to add a whole workshop manuscript here so it can be used as a reference piece for training design, something you can simply dive in and out of whenever you need it.

WITHOUT ANY MORE DELAY, HERE IS YOUR WORKSHOP MANUSCRIPT

First Slide

Why are we here?

Welcome to today's workshop, where we will embark on a collective journey to explore the world of open data. Our goal is to demystify this concept and understand how it can be leveraged strategically by public servants to drive social action and build resilient neighborhoods.

During our time together, we will not only learn about open data but also focus on effectively communicating its value to community groups and colleagues. It's crucial that we bridge the gap between the tech-savvy individuals who already grasp open data and the third sector, which often lacks awareness in this area despite being experts in our communities.

We must break down the barriers that hinder the adoption of open data, which can sometimes be perceived as overly academic or exclusive.

By the end of this workshop, you'll gain a comprehensive understanding of why open data is essential for everyone and how it can bring about positive change.

Change Slide

What is open data?

Open data is the foundation of transparency and accessibility, promoting the sharing and replication of information. It encompasses a wide range of data sources, including those released by tech giants, charities, transportation systems, healthcare institutions, and government entities.

When governments make specific information public, it becomes open government data (OGD) or "gov data." This initiative aims to demonstrate transparency, foster engagement with citizens, organizations, and businesses, and enhance government services through public scrutiny.

For example, housing data, environmental statistics, transportation information, election records, and various other datasets are utilized by government organizations. This data can be in the form of documents, PDFs, HTML files, or comprehensive Excel spreadsheets, depending on its nature.

Open data provides valuable insights into different aspects of our lives, ranging from traffic and environmental issues to healthcare indicators and population statistics. It enables us to access geographically specific data, such as school locations, playgrounds, or electric charging stations.

Later in the workshop, we will delve deeper into the technical aspects of making data open. Additionally, we'll address the concern that certain datasets may be challenging to find, emphasizing the importance of advocating for openness and applying gentle pressure where necessary.

Change Slide

The Power of Disruption

In our ever-changing world, disruptors play a crucial role in driving progress. They possess the ability to identify shortcomings, think creatively, and deconstruct social issues or broken civic systems. By removing ineffective elements and replacing them with innovative solutions, disruptors contribute to positive change.

This process involves envisioning alternatives and finding practical solutions, rather than focusing solely on aesthetics. While creating a visually appealing outcome is a bonus, the primary objective is to make things work and transform our neighborhoods into greener, more sustainable places. The value lies in solving problems and generating tangible results that improve our communities.

Change Slide

Open Data for All

Understanding open data does not require specialized technical knowledge. Unfortunately, the marketing and communication surrounding open data often employ complex, technocratic language, creating a sense of exclusion among potential users. This is particularly true for third-sector organizations, which struggle to resonate with the concept.

To engage and empower NGOs, we need to reframe our communication approach. When discussing open data with activists or community workers, highlighting its relevance to specific causes is crucial. For example, instead of emphasizing its importance for smart cities or Internet of Things projects, focus on how open data can support environmental campaigns or provide insights into sustainable heating solutions.

Open data should be accessible and usable for everyone, irrespective of their technical expertise. This workshop aims to facilitate conversations that make open data more comprehensible to non-profit staff and changemakers. We value your input and encourage active participation to collectively foster understanding and utilization of open data.

Change Slide

Basing Our Work on Evidence

To drive meaningful change, our arguments must be supported by solid evidence. Depending on the social issue at hand, data availability may vary. Climate activists, for instance, often have access to abundant environmental data. Conversely, accessing local data held by the government may pose challenges for organizations focused on specific communities.

As a collective, we must demonstrate the necessity and demand for open data. By showcasing the value of open data in addressing social issues, we can place it on the political agenda. People need to grasp the implications of these challenges in a language that resonates with them, supported by evidence that reflects their reality.

While open data is instrumental in influencing decision-making, engaging stakeholders, and securing funding, we should also recognize its potential to enhance the capacity of our organizations, campaigns, and projects. It helps demonstrate the need for support, generate awareness, and attract funding.

Change Slide

Sharing Data for Social Change

Data sharing is fundamental for effective social change, enabling coordinated and coherent responses. By sharing data, we inform policy, acquire funding, broaden impact, and engage new audiences. It allows us to understand the challenges we face, map social trends, and collaboratively work toward a sustainable future.

It's worth noting that data sharing goes beyond numerical values and technical formats. Third-sector organizations often possess valuable information in the form of surveys and community engagement data, which can contribute to our understanding of social trends. We'll explore the legal aspects and the process of making data open later in the workshop.

Question: When you collect data, do you ever consider sharing it?

Change Slide

Open Data for Social Action

Now, let's explore the possibilities that open data offers for social action.

Change Slide

The Importance of Third-Sector Engagement

Open data may be widely utilized by local businesses, analysts, and educational and health institutions, but it is the third sector that holds significant potential to effect change at the neighborhood level. We must prioritize efforts to encourage third-sector organizations to leverage the information made available through open data.

Releasing open data can simplify our lives by empowering communities to engage with us and contribute to improving public services. Moreover, it can aid in securing funding for local projects. Third-sector organizations possess specialized knowledge of the issues affecting our communities as they work and live within them. By utilizing open data, they can address these issues effectively. Additionally, their data collection efforts can shed light on critical issues and provide valuable insights.

For instance, a resident group living in an area with high pollution levels may leverage traffic data to raise awareness and exert pressure on local officials to take action. Similarly, a local chamber of commerce can utilize job data to highlight skill shortages and apply for funding to attract new industries to the region. Countless scenarios exist, and it's essential to consider the possibilities that open data presents.

Change Slide

So why does this workshop exist? This training has been formulated from on-the-ground research with governments and third-sector staff across the world. Here are the themes that were found.

Change Slide

Government workers

Although most do, a lot of staff didn't actually understand what open data is and were afraid to ask questions because they felt they should already know what it is and what to do with it, meaning the messages they were putting out via their own Council colleagues and thus the wider community were getting a muddy narrative.

This isn't a staff member's fault; it is the ultra-technocratic language that's been projected onto them. We can all get dazzled by snazzy words, and we all want to be as innovative as possible.

Change Slide

Charity, community, and voluntary staff

Most staff felt like they couldn't grasp what open data is because the language around it seemed too academic, which they did not understand nor identify with—and I hate to say it, but a lot of workers, especially those from community groups and tenant and resident associations, already have a mild distrust of local government and if they are presented with jargon-laced speeches, they will just think it's hyperbole and ignore it.

It's very important when we are explaining something, especially when it is about digitalization. It is very clear because, let's face it, it is confusing enough.

How do you feel? Does this resonate with you? What are your experiences?

Change Slide

Why is it important to bring community groups to the table?

There is no secret science here; it is easy to encourage them to use more open data for social good; you just tell them clearly and concisely how it is useful to them.

I'm going to go through some points about how each of these will support them, but also how it can impact us.

After these points, I want you to ask yourself: if you were a local third-sector officer and it was explained to you in this manner, would this pick up your interest?

If so, perhaps this could help you when you are either trying to explain it to colleagues who work with the community groups or if you are engaging with them yourselves.

This brings us to our next point...

Change Slide

Is open data even more important to our community organizations and can we learn from the pandemic?

Many NGOs ceased trading during the pandemic. This was because a lot of them depended on local government commissioning when budgets were cut or priorities shifted due to more investment in mental health services, for example. So with less money going around and even more priorities than ever before, it is more important than ever that NGOs are aware of any capacity-building tools out there that can aid them, and open data is one of those they can use it for.

You will have noticed funding has been mentioned a lot in the last few slides, which is on purpose as that is what we want you to lock in. Finally, keeping that in mind, if you were to explain how community organizations could use open data in a short burst, you could use the following points:

Funding—as a base of evidence for the need
Reporting, mapping, and monitoring social trends
Blogging and journalism (social action)
Holding decision-makers accountable

For a community to be resilient, they need these organizations, even more so after COVID-19 so if education can be an aid, let's use that.

Change Slide

The problem with open data

One of the issues with open data is that it is presented in a scientific way that has connotations that it is highly intellectual, which makes sense to business analysts, technologists, and most software developers.

But it is not exactly an inclusive approach, and that has created somewhat of a divide, and you don't need to be a rocket scientist to figure out what isn't going to attract activists or NGOs without some sort of strategy.

The idea of open data was coined as a social activist tool to improve collaboration between changemakers in the science community, but from that point, we have seemed to lose our way a little as, over time, the image of open data has been molded in a very technocratic way by business and tech professionals, which meant the narrative took on a very corporate slant that stuck and has not been able to shake it.

Business and corporate entities have a big interest in open data, and as that could be a good thing some of the time, that influence has had a sway on the way it is marketed; it can have some pretty sleek branding, which is why a lot of government data projects have words such as factory, corridor, or catapult attached to them when they are named, as that has business connotations.

That is not attractive to third-sector staff, and it actually turns them off as that language doesn't resonate, and they definitely feel that it is something not even remotely open to them.

If the current open data image was a person, it'd be a guy standing on a small stage in an expensive suit with an earpiece attached to his head. Nobody wants to be that guy, so let's not be that guy!

The thing is, as we touched on earlier in the course, that genuinely puts the community and volunteers off from even exploring what open data is because they feel they can't get on board with the message.

Change Slide

Let's spend a little time on how we can make data that we might have open. This might be a bit high-brow, and I'll try to be as clear as possible. A lot of this you will need to take away and run your own research, but here are some of the rules and mechanisms you need to consider if it is ever of interest.

Quick question: are you in the third sector? What data do you think you have that may be useful open data, especially in social action?

Change Slide

Making Your Data Open

Making your data open involves following certain rules and mechanisms. While we can only touch on the basics here, it's essential to conduct further research to fully understand the process. Let's explore some key considerations:

1. **Data Licensing:** Determine the appropriate license for your data. Creative Commons licenses are commonly used for open data, allowing others to use, share, and build upon your work while ensuring proper attribution.
2. **Data Formats:** Choose accessible and widely used formats for your data, such as CSV, JSON, or XML. Avoid proprietary formats that may limit accessibility.
3. **Data Quality:** Ensure the accuracy, completeness, and reliability of your data. Providing high-quality data enhances its usefulness and credibility.

4. **Privacy and Anonymization:** Assess any potential privacy concerns and anonymize sensitive information when sharing data. Protecting individuals' privacy is essential.
5. **Data Documentation:** Document your data comprehensively, including metadata that describes its structure, source, and context. Clear documentation helps others understand and effectively use the data.
6. **Data Accessibility:** Make your data easily accessible through online platforms or repositories. Consider user-friendly interfaces and APIs that enable efficient data retrieval.
7. **Data Governance:** Establish governance policies to ensure data consistency, security, and compliance with relevant regulations. This includes determining data ownership and responsibilities.

These are just some of the key aspects to consider when making your data open. It's crucial to assess the specific requirements and regulations that apply to your organization and data type.

Question: As a third-sector organization, what data do you think you have that could be valuable as open data for social action? How might this data support your work and initiatives?

Change Slide

Building Trust and Collaboration
Transparency and collaboration are vital for successful open data initiatives. To build trust and encourage collaboration, consider the following:

1. **Engage Stakeholders:** Involve your community and stakeholders from the beginning. Seek their input, understand their needs, and co-create solutions that address local challenges.
2. **Communication and Outreach:** Use clear, non-technical language to explain the benefits of open data and how it can support social action. Tailor your message to resonate with different audiences, including community organizations, activists, and volunteers.
3. **Capacity Building:** Provide training and resources to empower individuals and organizations to effectively use open data. This may include workshops, webinars, or online tutorials.
4. **Collaborative Platforms:** Foster collaboration through online platforms, forums, or data-sharing communities. Encourage knowledge exchange, problem-solving, and the sharing of best practices.
5. **Partnerships:** Establish partnerships with other organizations, including government agencies, academic institutions, and businesses. Collaborative efforts can amplify the impact of open data initiatives.

Remember, open data is not an end in itself but a means to achieve social action and positive change. By actively engaging with stakeholders, building trust, and fostering collaboration, you can leverage the power of open data to address community challenges and create a more resilient society.

Change Slide

In this section, we will cover:

1. The basics of opening your data
2. Licensing your data as "open data"
3. Steps to publishing your "open data"

Change Slide

Opening Your Data
  Before releasing your data, it's crucial to ensure compliance with the legal, ethical, disciplinary, and commercial requirements of your institution's policy and country's laws.
  Adhere to the terms and conditions under which you accessed the data, which may include safeguarding rules for surveys, for example.

Change Slide

Now, let's delve into the process. You might already possess valuable data, such as survey evidence, local information, workshop feedback, or people's thoughts.
  Please bear in mind that while some technical aspects will be discussed, the main points will be understandable to all. No need to worry about a test!

Change Slide

Understanding Open Data Formats
  Open data can be presented in two main formats: human-readable and machine-readable.
  Human-readable formats are easily understood by the naked eye, such as PDF, XML, and Doc. These files include reports, database documents, surveys, and photographs.
  Machine-readable data, on the other hand, is designed for computers to process efficiently. These formats, like CSV, JSON, and XML, may appear complex and require coding skills or specialized software for interpretation.
  While CSV and XML are primarily machine-readable, they can also be opened in spreadsheet software, making them more accessible to humans.

Change Slide

Common Recommendations for Open Data
  Consider the following recommendations when making your data open:

1. Align with Institutional Practices: Ensure your data complies with your institution's best practices.
2. Open Access: Make the data available to anyone without restrictions.
3. Reusability: Allow others to reuse and build upon your data if needed.
4. Anonymization: Remove any identifiers, such as names, postcodes, or birthdates, from the dataset to protect privacy.

Change Slide

Collecting Data: Methods and Types

But to make data "open," you need to know how to collect it or use what we have already got.

Data collection is an important step in gathering information for open data initiatives. Let's explore some easy methods to collect data and the different types you can gather:

Change Slide

Methods of Data Collection:

1. **Surveys:** Surveys are a simple way to gather information from people. Create questionnaires using online tools like Google Forms or SurveyMonkey. Share the survey through email, social media, or in-person conversations.
2. **Interviews:** Interviews involve talking to individuals or groups to learn about their experiences or opinions. You can conduct interviews face-to-face, over the phone, or online using platforms like Zoom or Skype.
3. **Observations:** Observations allow you to watch and record what's happening around you. Pay attention to behaviors, events, or phenomena, and jot down your observations.
4. **Existing Reports and Documents:** Look for reports or documents already available to the public that contain relevant information. Extract and compile data from these sources to contribute to the open data landscape.

Change Slide

Types of data to collect:

1. **Numbers and Measurements:** Collect data that involves numbers, such as counting the number of people attending an event or measuring the temperature at different locations.
2. **Stories and Experiences:** Gather qualitative data by listening to people's stories and experiences. Record their perspectives, opinions, or personal narratives to provide a deeper understanding of a topic.

3. **Locations and Maps:** Geospatial data involves capturing information tied to specific places. Note the locations where events occur or use GPS devices to record coordinates.
4. **Trends Over Time:** Collect data that shows how things change over time. This could be tracking monthly sales figures, monitoring website traffic, or recording population statistics over several years.

Change Slide

Tips for Easy Data Collection:

1. **Start with Clear Goals:** Define what you want to achieve with your data collection efforts. Have a clear purpose in mind to guide your process.
2. **Use Simple Tools:** Choose user-friendly tools like online survey platforms or smartphone apps to make data collection easier.
3. **Ask Clear Questions:** Keep survey questions simple and easy to understand. Avoid jargon or technical terms that might confuse participants.
4. **Collect Data from a Small Group:** If your target audience is large, consider starting with a small group to practice your data collection skills before scaling up.
5. **Respect Privacy:** Make sure to obtain consent when collecting personal data, and ensure that any sensitive information remains confidential and secure.

Change Slide

Collecting data for open data initiatives can be simple, even if you have little experience. Use methods like surveys, interviews, and observations, and leverage existing reports. Collect different types of data, such as numbers, stories, locations, and trends. Follow these tips to make the data collection process easier and respect privacy. Your efforts will contribute to the growing open data community.

Change Slide

Principles for Making Your Data Open
    Now, let's discuss the key principles to consider when opening your data:

Change Slide

Completeness: If exporting raw datasets, such as Excel or machine-readable files, ensure they are as complete as possible. Provide accompanying metadata, formulas, and explanations for data calculations. This enables users to understand the data thoroughly.

Change Slide

Primary Sources: Clearly indicate and reference the sources from which your data was collected.

Change Slide

Timeliness: Release data in a reasonable timeframe, especially if it is time-dependent.

Change Slide

Accessibility: Make your datasets easily accessible to users. Accessibility refers to the ease with which information can be obtained.

Change Slide

Machine Readability: If your data is handwritten, consider using Optical Character Recognition (OCR) to convert it into machine-readable text. Avoid releasing handwritten data, as it is not easily accessible. Provide notes on the recommended software for accessing the data.

Change Slide

Open Standards: Use open standards when formatting your datasets. Ensure the file can be opened using various programs rather than proprietary software. For example, instead of relying on Microsoft Excel, consider using freely available formats that don't require a license.

Change Slide

Licensing Your Data

Licensing is a crucial step in making your data open. To be considered open data, it must be licensed appropriately. The most common approach is to use Creative Commons licenses, which allow for free distribution of the work while retaining copyright and requiring attribution.

Creative Commons licenses simplify the legal aspects, but it's also worth exploring if your local government has its own open licenses. In most cases, sticking with Creative Commons licenses is recommended.

Change Slide

Pathways to Release Your Data

To release your data, follow these steps:

1. Choose the dataset you intend to make open, ensuring identities are removed and the data is simplified.
2. Apply an open license to the dataset, using Creative Commons licenses or suitable alternatives.
3. Publish your data, either through platforms like ckan.org (an open-source data management tool) or on your own website if you have the technical capability.
4. Promote and showcase your data by sharing it on the web and organizing a central catalog on your website.

Change Slide

Collecting Data and Making It Open: Legal Considerations
    Introduction:
    If you're new to data collection and the concept of open data, this section will guide you through the process while ensuring legal compliance and protecting sensitive information. Let's explore the steps involved:

Change Slide

Step 1: Determine Your Data Collection Needs

Before collecting data, clearly define your goals and the type of information you require. Consider the purpose of the data, whether it aligns with your organization's objectives, and the potential benefits of making it open.

Change Slide

Step 2: Choose an Appropriate Data Collection Method

Select a data collection method that suits your needs and resources. Common methods include surveys, interviews, observations, and online forms. Ensure that the method you choose is legal and aligns with data protection regulations in your jurisdiction.

Change Slide

Step 3: Design a Simple Data Collection Form

When creating a data collection form, keep it simple and user-friendly, especially if you're new to this process. Use a spreadsheet tool, such as Microsoft Excel or Google

Sheets, to design your form. Include only the necessary fields to gather the information you need, and avoid collecting sensitive or personally identifiable information unless absolutely necessary.

Change Slide

Step 4: Obtain Informed Consent

If your data collection involves individuals, obtain informed consent from participants. Clearly explain the purpose of the data collection, how it will be used, and any potential risks or benefits. Ensure that participants understand their rights and provide them with the option to withdraw their consent at any time.

Change Slide

Step 5: Anonymize or De-identify Data

To protect privacy and comply with data protection regulations, anonymize or de-identify your data before making it open. Remove any information that can directly or indirectly identify individuals, such as names, addresses, or unique identifiers. This step ensures that personal privacy is preserved while enabling the data to be shared openly.

Change Slide

Step 6: Choose an Appropriate Open Data License

Select an open data license to govern the use and distribution of your data. Creative Commons licenses, such as CC0 (Creative Commons Zero) or CC-BY (Creative Commons Attribution), are commonly used for open data. These licenses allow others to freely access, use, and build upon your data while ensuring proper attribution and compliance with legal requirements.

Change Slide

Step 7: Publish Your Data in a Secure Manner

When publishing your data, consider using a reputable open data platform or your organization's website. Ensure that the platform or website provides secure data hosting and access controls. This helps protect the data from unauthorized access while allowing others to discover and access the open data easily.

Change Slide

By following these steps, you can collect data in a legal and ethical manner and make it open for others to use and benefit from. Remember to prioritize data privacy, obtain informed consent, and choose an appropriate open data license. With the right approach, you can contribute to the open data movement and empower others with valuable information.

Change Slide

Workshop Summary

Thank you for joining us in this workshop on open data. Let's recap what we have learned and explore some recommendations for future action.

Change Slides

Key Takeaways

Open data promotes transparency and accessibility, enabling the sharing and replication of information across various sectors.

It is crucial to bridge the gap between tech-savvy individuals and the third sector to ensure widespread understanding and adoption of open data.

Open data empowers communities, enhances decision-making, and drives positive social change.

Change Slides

Recommendations for Action

Running Your Own Events: Organize events or workshops within your organization or community to educate and engage others about open data. Tailor the content to resonate with your audience and highlight its relevance to specific causes.

Developing an Open Data Strategy or Policy: Create a comprehensive strategy or policy for open data within your organization or community group. Define goals, identify data sources, determine licensing and formatting standards, and establish guidelines for data quality and privacy.

Advocacy for Openness: Advocate for openness in data across government entities and institutions. Encourage the release of data relevant to your cause and apply gentle pressure when necessary.

Collaboration and Partnerships: Seek opportunities for collaboration with other organizations, including government agencies, academic institutions, and businesses. By working together, you can leverage each other's strengths and amplify the impact of open data initiatives.

Capacity Building: Provide training and resources to empower individuals and organizations to effectively use open data. Conduct workshops, webinars, or online tutorials to enhance data literacy and utilization skills.

Data Sharing for Social Change: Embrace data sharing to foster coordinated and coherent responses to social issues. By sharing data, you can inform policy, acquire funding, broaden impact, and engage new audiences.

Change Slides

Embracing Open Data for Resilient Communities

Open data is not just a buzzword; it's a tool for creating resilient communities. By leveraging open data strategically, we can address social challenges, drive positive change, and empower individuals and organizations to make informed decisions.

Change Slides

Thank You!

Thank you for your active participation in this workshop. We hope you gained valuable insights and felt inspired to explore open data further. Remember, together, we can create a more transparent, inclusive, and resilient society.

Printed in the United States
by Baker & Taylor Publisher Services